A FATHER'S STORY

ROY F. WEAVER

MARIE A FATHER'S STORY
Copyright © 2026 by Roy F. Weaver

Paperback: 979-8-9942746-0-6
Ebook: 979-8-9942746-1-3

5 out of 5 stars Excellant read!
This book was enthralling. Once I started, I couldn't put it down. Sad on one hand, made me smile on the other. A true testament straight from a father's heart for a daughter who was taken way too soon. I know Marie is Raisin' Hell in Heaven waiting on her Dad to dance thru those gates!!
—*Cteal, Amazon Reviews*

5 out of 5 stars Longing for someone..
Marie: A Father's Story is such a wonderful book that tells a ones lifetime as a son I can feel how Roy Weaver felt while writing the book. In this instance, my father used to do what Roy did to Marie upon reading it I felt the love and longing of a father for his daughter it is such a wonderful story indeed.
—*Andrew M., Amazon Reviews*

5 out of 5 stars Stay on track don't be in such a hurry
The lesson that Roy Weaver trying to portray is that there is a beginning and end of one's lifetime and he clearly states that you should not hurry and enjoy the scenery in every day that passes in your life. The book is so meaningful and has the capability of making your mood uplift and rethink that life is such a wonderful gift we should enjoy it with moderation. It was a wonderful book kudos to Roy Weaver
—*Noah, Amazon Reviews*

Introduction

Hello, I am going to tell you a story about an extraordinary young lady. Marie is no longer gracing us with her vibrant personality and infectious smile. She has been gone for some time now. Her name has faded from the lips of those she cast her shining light upon and, in some cases, turned their world completely upside down, inside out, and sideways. My grandfather developed Alzheimer Dementia, my father succumbed to Alzheimer Dementia, now I am starting to forget more than I remember. Except for the vivid images from my time in Iraq and the precious moments among all the chaos that was "Marie". The only name you will see in my story is Marie's because this is her story. As for me, I am writing her story through tears, smiles, joy, sadness, some regret but mostly love. This is my "Notebook".

"First there is a God, then there is no God, then there is"

She was born Lindsy Marie on August 28th, 1979, at 4:46 PM in Green Bay, Wisconsin. The name Lindsy after Lindsay Wagner, the Bionic Woman, and "Marie" after her great Aunt Marie. Her mother insisted on calling her Lindsy. I preferred to call her Marie. I believe even Marie preferred Marie. Simply because I was the one who took her to the trinket store to find a Keychain with her name on it. Try to find Lindsy without the "e" or "a". So, Marie it was whenever she was around me. She also had a five-pound keychain tagged with every quippy little quote she found amusing.

Her great aunt Marie's life was coming to an end after a long struggle with cancer. She fought so hard, but the cancer had metastasized throughout her frail body. At the same time, little Lindsy Marie was anxiously preparing to come into the world.

She arrived just in time to meet her Great Aunt before she passed. Marie's projected arrival was already causing some stress for her mother and me. She was ten days past due. After what seemed like an eternity waiting to meet this kid, it finally happened.

One afternoon as I was preparing to leave the house on my way to work, I grabbed her mother from behind and shook her up and down. Then off I went to my 3:00 – 11:00 P.M. shift as night custodian at Bay View Middle School. Apparently, the up and down nudging did the trick. I got "The" phone call at work around 4:30 P.M. that contractions were about seven to eight minutes apart. By 10:00 P.M. we were in the preplanned comfort of the labor and delivery room. Soft lighting, comfortable chair, a bag lunch and peanut M&Ms for me. As things go, things never go as planned. The first nurse who checked us in was ending her shift. She introduced us to the next shift nurse, who wasn't there when we were given the in-service on how things would go. My first issue was why wasn't anyone responding when I ring this little bell. Even though I graduated from

Labor coaching class with honors, I was not ready to be doing this by myself.

It was going to be a 26-hour ordeal getting to finally meet Marie. Contractions, back labor, eight hours of hard labor, drugs, no drugs, ice chips, trips to the bathroom, pacing, and chasing down nurses. I could only ring that little bell so many times waiting for the Nurse to assist in resolving one crisis or another. I thought maybe throwing the little bell out into the hallway might help. Nope, not the best idea. Worst of all, her mother's water wouldn't break because Marie's head was up against the door. Marie was trying to push her way out along with her yet to be broken water filled room.

Another nurse's shift went by. Then the next nurse's shift. The one that always says things like "you got yourself into this". Then the possibility of the next Doctor's shift. After a few comments between doctor and nurse, like "Should I give her a pain blocker?" followed by "kind of late now isn't it", the doctor was able to break through the inner sanctum and insistently, little 7 lb. 6 oz Lindsy Marie pushed her way into the world. Obviously pissed off about something or another. Probably because our less than favorite nurse of the three shifts gave her less than a perfect 10 for not sticking the landing. I should have seen that as a sign of things to come.

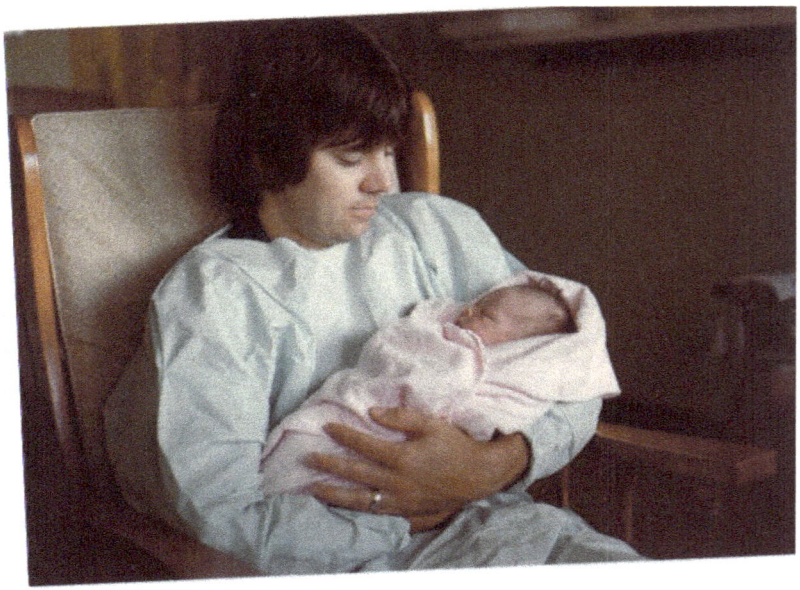

For the next three months, her mother and I worked different shifts. I would be home with Marie from 6:00 until 2:00 during the day. Her mom would be alone with Lindsy from 3:00 to 11:00. It seemed Marie would only stop screaming when I held her face down draped over my forearm. She was colicky, so they all said.

Marie's "never take no for an answer" attitude would never let up. Her 26 hours of struggling to come into this world would be followed by the next 26 years fighting with all she had against any bully or institution if she thought for a minute something wasn't fair. After 26 years Marie would begin her four-year fight with an enemy, I knew was going to eventually defeat her, even though she wasn't so convinced.

What I didn't know at the time was that Marie would become that person we all want to be, and often that person we sometimes would love to avoid. Every social situation would present some issue regarding some injustice. There was going to be some kind of confrontation in her life. How many of us simply accept not getting exactly what we ask for or just settle with less than our expectations? If it wasn't fair or wasn't right Marie was going to try to make it right. At the very least let everyone know it wasn't right. I can say all this now. Back then I was clueless. From that day on there were no more little bells to ring for help. I would refer to her demanding, do it or else negotiating style, as her "Grandpa gene". Yes, her grandfather was near as dammit the same personality. The one who puts the cop on the stand in court over a traffic ticket and wins.

Marie would live the rest of her life moving from place to place; Starting in Green Bay, Wisconsin where she was born, to Kennesaw, Georgia, to Biloxi, Mississippi, to Dale City, Virginia, to Sacramento, California, to Atlanta, Georgia, to Bealeton, Virginia, to Eatontown, New Jersey, back to Atlanta, to Seattle, Washington, back to Atlanta, again to Green Bay, and eventually Colorado Springs, Colorado. She was always trying to adapt to new schools, new jobs, new friends, new climate, and of course, new enemies. Not always with people. Sometimes with the differences in regional cultures and stubborn ideals or philosophies. I was never quite sure if this was her journey or mine and she was driving the train.

Three and a half months after Marie was born, we left Green Bay for a better climate, and to leave my past behind. I grew up in Green Bay, Marie's mother did not. That's all I will say for now. We moved to Kennesaw, Georgia, with a new baby, a dog named Pepper, and a blue parakeet named Tweet. Only one flat tire in the middle of the night in the mountains of Tennessee, and we moved in with Nanny and Pappa.

Papa found me a job as a Nailer on a framing crew. I rode the Honda 350 motorcycle my dad gave me around the I-285 beltway from Kennesaw to Buckhead every morning at 0600, to drive nails, haul lumber, stack bricks and wade in shin-deep cement as it poured out the back end of a cement truck into the piers and footings of the 250 ft long apartment buildings we were building. Occasionally I was on the roof nailing down plywood and dodging a sheet or two that one of my crew mates threw above me so it would slide down the roof making me jump over it. It was thirty feet to the ground. I was from Wisconsin working on a tobacco spitting redneck framing crew in Georgia.

After a few months of getting welfare milk and cereal, with no health insurance, I asked Papa about his career in the Air Force. It was a no brainer. I joined the Air Force. Six weeks at Lackland Air Force Base for basic training then to Keesler Air Force Base in Biloxi, Mississippi for Tech School. We moved into a trailer park away from the base because I was married. They called us Separate Rats meaning we received additional housing and sustenance allowance.

Marie and I would always have a very special relationship. From the day she was born I held her in my arms and in my heart. She was undeniably Daddy's girl. She was my little Punkin. As she grew older, talking to her, even as a child, was like talking to a grown-up. All my friends couldn't believe how they could carry on a conversation with her.

We did so many activities together. From sports to schoolwork, to working on the car, or remodeling this old southern cottage we lived in after we moved out of the Trailer. She handed me wrenches whenever I was working on the car or van. She held the board or held the flashlight and handed me hammers, saws, and nails when I was building shelves, bookcases, her toy box, or a custom table for our custom window van. We played frisbee, she was in gymnastics, and later she played volleyball and softball in middle and high school.

When Marie was three years old, she was enrolled in a Montessori program at the AFB Chappel. She excelled at almost every aptitude. Which lead me to believe we would have a great successful lifetime education experience.

We hooked up a component stereo together after which she would dance in front of with the headphones on while singing along. A new program called MTV began showing on cable TV. Watching music videos all day and night was addicting. Especially with the audio wired from the TV directly to the stereo. Marie was especially fond of Stevie Nicks. We took her to a Stevie Nicks concert at the Gulf Coast Coliseum where she stood on the seats and sang along with every word.

We also watched football together. She loved the Green Bay Packers. We wrestled during games as if we were on the field trying to recover a fumble. Another show we liked was "Kung Fu". We played boxing and did Kung Fu fighting. I wanted her to be able to defend herself. I would let her hit me as hard as she could. Which was a benefit and a curse later in her life. I played quarterback for my Air Force Unit's flag football team, and I was the pitcher on the Keesler Air force Base fast-pitch softball team. Marie came to every one of my football and softball games while I was in the Air Force.

I decided to leave the Air force after four years and was recruited for a Defense Contracting job in Northern Virginia. We bought a house in Dale City where the streets all had "Dale" in the name. We lived on Kerrydale Court. Marie began her experience with Public School in Kindergarten at a school within walking distance from our home. It was called Kerrydale Grade School.

The transition from Montessori to public school presented some challenges for Marie. She hated the constant coloring. She knew her colors. She was already reading and writing. She would get bored and start chatting and socializing after she scribbled her entire page in one color. While playing with a neighbor kid she was pushed down on the sidewalk and broke both of her two front teeth. It would take nearly two Christmases for her adult teeth to finally grow in.

To keep her moving forward, I would let Marie shift my 1976 red Datsun pickup truck, or sit in my lap to steer, whenever I would go get building material for the house we bought. By the time she was ten it was my 1967 GTA Fastback restored Mustang. Of course, that only made her more anxious to get her own car when she turned sixteen. It was even better that she learned to drive a vehicle with a standard transmission, they are usually cheaper than automatic.

We only lived in Dale City for a year before I was transferred to Sacrament, California.

Aside from being a very active child. She was a lot of fun to be around between the ages of five to ten years old. Marie could also be very polite at that age. She often applied that skill to manipulating grownups, to achieve her desired outcome. Except for Grandpa, he saw right through it.

My parents divorced while I was in the Air Force. First, we were visited by Grandma and her new friend. We took them to party with us in New Orleans. Then came Grandpa with his new lady friend. Once again, we were off to New Orleans. I will never drink another Hurricane. That's also the time when Dad introduced me to the game of golf. That four letter word. Everywhere we lived. Grandpa would come with his new wife to play golf.

Marie loved music and she loved horses. She spent a lot of time with her mother going to the barn and taking care of the horses. Yes, we had a horse. Marie's mother was active in equestrian competitions. She had been taking lessons for a couple years before we were married.

My mother-in-law purchased a horse for Marie's mother when we got married. It was the dappled gray quarter horse she had been taking lessons with. We spent a lot of time at the barn and stables where we boarded the horse. I was always complaining about the time and money we spent at the equestrian complex for lessons, training, and horse shows.

We ultimately moved the horse to a privately owned smaller barn with just a couple horses for boarding only. Marie's mother could use their limited pasture to ride and train her own horse. Early one morning I received a phone call that the barn had burned to the ground, and it was a total loss. All the horses supposedly died in the barn fire. We didn't know that the owner was having financial issues.

They had all their furniture and belongings stored in the upper part of the barn while the horses were down below in the stalls. The incident suspiciously looked like the owners of the boarding stable sold the horses and set the fire for the insurance. We never did get to investigate whether the horses were in the barn at the time. They owners had it bulldozed over by the time we were allowed on the property to investigate. Our equestrian adventure would continue later in life after we moved to California.

If you are thinking it was all my fault for moving the horse to the barn that burned down, you may be right. So, of course it was an easy call to make. When I made enough money I would buy another horse, and a truck, and a trailer and find a stable for lessons and horse shows.

I was the Horse show dad. I drove the truck pulling the two-horse trailer when traveling to equestrian horse shows. Our thoroughbred bay mare was named Moon Shadow. The frame around our truck license plate read I'm being followed by a Moon Shadow.

Marie would take lessons on a white Shetland pony named Daisy.

One time, during a horse show, Marie's horse started acting up in the arena. Marie grabbed those reins and sternly regained her horse's composure. She was about seven years old at the time and loved riding Moon Shadow.

I also taught Marie to ride her bicycle while living in Sacramento. She had a propensity for running into streetlight poles. I thought maybe she had a balance issue with her brain. She eventually became one of the local kid's bicycle gangs and rode all over the dirt piles in the field next to our house.

The streetlights coming on meant coming home for dinner, then bath and time for bed. Well, one night she didn't come home when the streetlights came on. I went outside to check the regular play areas. I found her little bicycle just a few doors down the street, lying between the sidewalk and the curb. That was nothing less than bone chilling panic.

I didn't exactly trust the neighborhood to begin with. My own bicycle had been stolen from my porch and our house had been broken into with some expensive things stolen a few weeks earlier. Now my only child is missing. I ran into the house, yelled to her mother, and we were off to search the entire world if we had to. A brief door to door search resulted in finding Marie inside the neighbor's house playing like it was no big deal. This would not be the only time Marie's adventures sent me into panic mode.

While living in California Marie began her inquisitive journey to learn about religion and trying to understand about God, death, and her own spirituality. I encouraged Marie to expand her understanding of religion and spiritual beliefs by questioning everything anyone tells her about religion, death and the meaning of life. Marie would attend Sunday services with her friends and had a lot of questions because of the differences in how they worshipped or what they talked about. She didn't really commit to any dogmatic stuff. She simply enjoyed singing, especially at the more contemporary progressive services. She loved to sing and perform, which she did all the time with her keyboard and little neighborhood Girl Band.

Marie also enjoyed participating in Native American Indian cultural events and ceremonies. We would travel to different Pow Wows during our Indian Spiritual enrichment adventures. I think it was just something people did in California, given the rich history and heritage in that area. Marie was fascinated with going to Pow Wows. She loved the dancing, and we had many discussions about the parallels with other religions she experienced.

She started to ask more questions about dealing with death and what happens after we die. Marie's only experience with death at this point was when our dog Pepper developed cancer and we had her euthanized at the vet.

Marie grew up around dogs and horses and loved animals. She seemed to always have a dog or a cat or both. She got her own cat when she was about seven years old. K.C. for Kitty Cat. That cat would still be with her 20 years later. Another kitten jumped out from the shrubs while we were walking in the neighborhood. So, Marie had two cats. Cats were her playmates which worked out great for an only child. Her cats were always wearing doll clothes.

Some of our other family adventures in the great state of California, back then, included skiing in the Sierras. We hit the slopes at places like Squaw Valley, Sierra Ski Ranch and Heavenly ski resort.

We also loved camping in the giant Redwood trees along the Eel River in way up north California. We would sit by the fire at night and play Carlos Nakai flute music that permeated through the trees. Other campers would come looking for the Indians, expecting to see a real live Indian show. We also spent some time camping in Yosemite National Park. We went with a local Boy Scout Troop to hike up to the top of Mt. Dana. I was an Eagle scout and helped with the camping and hiking events. One of the scouts took a particular interest in Marie and fell all over himself helping her with gathering wood for the fire or taking walks through the trees and trails. Very cute when they are ten and not out looking for a hiding place to smoke.

Around the time Marie was eleven years old we sent her back to Georgia to stay with her Grandparents, Nanny and

Papa. Our marriage was falling apart. I had a very peculiar job on a program that was not to be discussed with or questioned by even members of my family. Including my own wife. That led to some very challenging issues including suspicions about where I was going and what I was doing when I would just leave for a couple weeks. We sold the horse, the truck, and the trailer. Everything else was packed up into a United moving truck and off to Georgia it went. Marie was devastated by mine and her mother's divorce. I hated to see her leave, but I knew I could not win a custody fight in the state of California. I had to sell the mustang. After two months of flat tires on my bicycle from riding over needly like weed burs on the way to work, I recovered enough to purchase a Dodge Raider pickup truck. As I was leaving work, I noticed a flyer at the guard shack for country dance lessons. What the heck, I was off on a new adventure in my social life. It would be something Marie and I could do if we ever got back together.

Meanwhile back in Georgia, Marie began acting out her displeasure over not having a say in the decision. Like a lot of divorced kids, she started hanging out with older kids who would impair her judgement. Friends, especially friends plus alcohol, and a car, will impair your judgement.

After a year of living across the country from Marie, I was eventually able to transfer my job from Sacramento, California to Augusta, Georgia. I would be much closer to Marie. About three years back and forth between Augusta and Kennesaw visiting her, and her visiting me, she grew very rebellious and eventually became unmanageable for her mother.

Sneaking out of the house, taking off in cars with older boys after school, and hanging out down by the river.

She was just turning thirteen years old when her mother decided Marie should be with her dad for a while. At least until she became an adult. I got custody of Marie and her cat K.C. Her mother got the other cat, which was named LC for Little Cat, in case you were wondering. Marie's mother packed her up in a U-Haul truck and I met them halfway for the exchange. I guess you could say they had their own little divorce. I thought, great, no more child support. Trust me, there are some situations where you can't pay enough for child support. Like the day Hell gets its wheels. So, I am now a single father about to take custody of a teen-aged daughter. She left her home and friends in Atlanta, moved in with me in Augusta, and within a few months we were going to move again to Virginia. What could possibly go wrong? The good news was that she wasn't in school at the time.

I kept getting caught up in all the Base Realignment and Closure (BRAC) actions during those years. I may have the record for BRAC moves. The one activity that may have saved at least some of my connection with Marie was our interest in and participation in Country dancing. I made some great friends over the three years I spent in Augusta. We had become a big family. Cookouts together, traveling to compete and perform in dance shows, going out to local and distant Honky Tonks from Atlanta to Charlotte, NC and in between. We formed a show style dance team with matching shirts and everything. Country dancing and line dancing did a lot to save my relationship with Marie. Marie loved to dance and hang out with my adult friends and their kids. It was the closest thing to family the two of us would ever share. We all looked out for each other. Cookouts every weekend, dance lessons every Sunday at the community center, dance shows at the Fair, or moving along on a flatbed truck in a parade. Marie enjoyed performing and I loved to dance with her.

Even after moving to Virginia, we found another dance group and joined them in very similar activities. They were all adults though and were more about meeting at the dances than the family cookouts with volleyball, horseshoes, and archery kinds of activities.

I had become as close as a brother to one of my co-workers who also moved along with us from Augusta to Virginia because of BRAC. He had two daughters, one with the same first name as Marie. He went through a Divorce while in Virginia and moved in with us until he could find a place of his own. BRAC had a devastating effect on married couples and families. It was just bad to do that to people.

The two of us would go to Marie's volleyball games and cheer her on. She was totally embarrassed having two dad characters siting together in the bleachers cheering for her.

After a successful year of middle school in Virginia where Marie even participated in playing volleyball. We had somewhat of a normal home life. We watched a lot of NASCAR racing and practiced line dances with some dance friends that would come over. There was that incident at the roller-skating rink. But other than that Marie was getting along, except for a few episodes of out-of-control tantrums when she didn't get her way. To me that was normal.

She had to share a bathroom with our house guest for a while. That drove her crazy. Marie would start screaming at me about his bathroom habits and the toilet seat. The usual stuff, except that her eyes would turn dark, and she would appear to be in some kind of trance as if she were possessed. I would ask if she was brain damaged when her sense of reason would get so out of balance. We tried to be sensitive to her needs but my God she would go off and punch the walls in her room.

Marie's life, and of course mine too, got worse when she started High School. While in High School, she endured two years of constant bullying, fighting with other students, continuous excuses from the principal threatening to expel her, and teachers who claimed they weren't responsible for behavior problems outside of classroom.

Marie struggled in school and became very isolated because no one else would accept her in their clique. I guess it is the law of attraction that draws this type of activity to certain people. When we first moved from Georgia to Virginia and into our new house, Marie went to the roller-skating rink just up the road from where we lived. Of course, she met a boy, who apparently was the love interest of, you guessed it, the leader of the Mean Girl pack. She was also the daughter of a police officer. She just happened to have BOXRGRL as her personalized license plate. The principal, and close friend of the School Security Officer insisted that BOXRGRL, the daughter of a police officer, wouldn't do those things, nor encourage her entourage to bully Marie like that. He claimed he knew all those girls since they were in grade school. So, I asked, then how did they end up on Marie's back pounding her in the head on her way to lunch? Only one excuse, Marie must be doing something to incite them. Yah, she talked to a boy.

Marie did, however, gain the trust and friendship of a couple of other girls that had been bullied prior to her arrival. Now Marie had her own clique. They were often at the house telling me their side of the many stories. Yes, I engaged, and yes revenge comes later. I just didn't want her to give up on school. I made her promise not to fight back. How do you think that went?

The bullying continued between classes, and whenever Marie would be in the hallway near the infamous cafeteria. Crowded hallway, lots of commotion, hit and run. Marie didn't always hold back. She was trying really hard to do as I asked and trust me that we would get it resolved. Every time she fought back, she would get a three-day vacation. Just about the time Marie was going to be expelled from school for good, we would finally get our day in court. It seems to be a family trait to end up in court when dealing with these types of issues. I wrote letters to the school Board and letters to the principal, because I am a writer. I wanted to make sure I documented the chronological event history.

Being a single parent was difficult as I had to trust Marie with staying home after school until I got home from work.

Two of my new co-workers lived across the road, I call it a road because it was gravel. They had no children and liked Marie. They were always available to assist Marie if she ever needed help with something and I wasn't there. We also had other neighbors living catty corner across the road. These neighbors were very observant of the activities in my house. It was not unusual to come home from work and find Marie yelling obscenities across the road at the observant neighbors. One day I came home to find a giant middle finger snow sculpture in the front yard facing the house across the road. Of course, it got extremely cold that night and the "Finger" as we called it, became solid ice and didn't melt for a month. It was quite detailed down to the lines in the knuckles and had a perfect thumbnail. I made her add the extra knuckles because it looked like something else at first.

When Marie turned 16, she got a driver's license. Remembering how much we enjoyed working on cars together, I bought a white 1965 Dodge Dart from my boss. We were going to make it a project car that we could work on together. I did make her learn to change a tire and jump start a car before I would let her get a license. Now she could get to school without walking to the bus stop. The bus stop seemed to be where many of the fighting incidents occurred. Several more incidents would break out during lunchtime where she was being bullied again.

One day Marie let her friend drive her Hooptie, as she called it, and they got into an accident. No one was hurt thankfully and It was the other driver's fault. The Hooptie had no damage, but it destroyed the other plastic car.

Her nice white car had also been tagged, as the kids called it, with blue spray paint. I made her scrub almost down to the primer to get the blue spray paint off the hood and doors. Good thing we waxed it because the paint did rub off. I would have preferred toilet paper in the trees, quite frankly.

I explained to Marie that I was being patient and wanted her to try to avoid fighting in school, at the bus stop, in town, at the roller rink, and all the usual places if she could. She didn't have any allies from the teachers and staff, especially the school security officer. We waited until BOXRGRL finally turned 18. We charged her with a vehicular assault charge after she ran Marie off the road after she got off the school bus. Luckily Marie had a friend and witness with her that day. BOXRGRL's under-aged followers jumped out of the car, pushed Marie to the ground, and beat on her in the ditch along the side of the road.

Amazingly enough, after explaining the situation to the district Magistrate, who also knew these girls since grade school, he agreed to pursue the charges. We finally got to talk to someone who had a different opinion than the principal, the school board, and especially the school security officer. BOXRGRL was the daughter of a police officer, she agreed to apologize to Marie and to me. She received a one year suspended jail sentence for harassing and threatening behavior, to include vehicular assault. She promised that Marie would not be harassed and bullied any more.

Marie became sort of a hero for standing up to and eventually taking down the bullies. Marie often stepped in to defend her fellow victims from the bullying. She no longer had anything to lose. The long and arduous process of fighting through the legal system, while Marie and her friends were being harassed and assaulted, ended with less than satisfactory justice compared to the pain and suffering Marie had to endure. I wanted to take down the entire administration.

When a teenager loses trust in an institution there are extreme consequences. It was almost too late for an unskilled single parent in my predicament to save the situation. Marie was already deep into the drugs and alcohol crowd I was afraid to leave her alone at home waiting for me to get there after work no matter how many neighbors I had watching the house. In fact, she was hardly ever alone. There would be wine and beer bottles not so discreetly hidden in the trash cans. Jewelry would be missing, and of course the toilet seat was always in the full upright position. I begged her to stop missing school. I even told her if she misses one more day, I was going to kick her ass. She had punched holes in the walls and a hole in her bedroom door, for which I believed she deserved an ass whooping anyway.

The school office lady called me at work after Marie had missed twenty-six days of school in a row. They were happy to inform me that Marie was being expelled. I asked why they didn't call me after she had missed two or three days. They said they were hoping to reach the magic number 26 so they could be done with her. I would go to work in the morning thinking she was going to school.

I had to stand on my promise that I would kick her ass, just like my own Dad used to do when we would commit far lesser offenses. Marie was ready though. She brought home a friend that recently had a baby. They were lounging in the downstairs living room watching TV. Now Marie had a witness in case the ass kicking was an actual physical ass kicking. So, I demonstrated the classic discipline technique we grew up with. Only I used my open hand instead of a leather belt to administer a good old-fashioned spanking.

As a result, Marie and her friend, baby in tow, ran out the door to the nosey neighbor's house, who of course called the police to report Domestic violence at my address. The girls then took off in a vehicle I suspected was driven by the Baby Daddy. I went to change my underwear while I waited for the police to arrive. I figured I was going to jail.

While I was waiting, a lady friend of mine from work stopped by. She happened to be the Ex-daughter-in-law of a retired local police detective. When the police showed up, they recognized her. They exchanged greetings and when she told them everything was fine, and we were just about to start dinner. Fortunately for me, they called in a false alarm and off they went. Probably due to the numerous calls that our neighbor had made in the past three years. She called her Ex-father-in-law, and we sat down to figure out what to do next. I eventually married that woman.

Now I have a 16-year-old missing, and she is on the run with a young girl and a baby. My new retired detective friend engaged some of his former detective friends and the resources of the local police in the search. Not BOXRGRL's dad. After about three days they found evidence that Marie, the baby and mother, and someone with a credit card, probably the baby Daddy, checked into the local Comfort Inn. It was the same Comfort Inn we stayed at while awaiting permanent residence in the house with the observant neighbors. I was relieved that they hadn't ended up in D.C., where some of Marie's drug dealer friends claimed to be from, before I chased them out of my house with the shotgun. They said Marie invited them there and they weren't going to leave, and I couldn't make them.

Back at the Comfort Inn, there was hair in the sink, hair dye packaging in the trash can, and the office clerk admitting that they were there within just a few hours. The search continued, to include the parent's residents of the girl with the baby. They always seem to want to go home when they know the cops are looking for them. Marie wasn't there. The young mother, the baby and the baby Dady were there at the house. Again, panic. The baby momma said Marie got into a car with some guy she called to pick her up. I wanted roadblocks set up on every route going to D.C. Any father would. But I knew that was not going to happen. Marie's trail suddenly went cold. It was three agonizing days thinking for sure she was lost in D.C. and would end up as a drug-addicted Prostitute on 14th Street. For just a split second I thought that Pimp has no idea what he's getting into.

Long story short, we received a phone call. I had friends from work that lived in town. Marie and my coworker's wife were close. She was a sort of Mother figure for Marie. She called me from their house in the morning after Marie had a chance to get some sleep and eat breakfast. My friends said she was in bad shape. Her face was all purple and swollen and she appeared to have some broken ribs. She said Marie was afraid of what I would do to her if she came home. That's why she went to their house to have them call me. I said "what, like the spanking I gave you was worse than the beating you got".

Apparently, she was with her 26-year-old drug dealer friend from D.C. when his entourage of female followers became jealous of little Marie. They proceeded to beat the ever-living crap out of her. They dragged her into the woods, where they dumped her. Marie said she fought back but there were too many of them. She eventually just played unconscious so they would stop kicking her in the face and ribs. She wanted them to leave so she could just lay there in the middle of the woods, in the middle of the night to die. When they finally did leave, Marie just laid there and cried until she drifted off to sleep or unconsciousness.

It was cold, dark, and very late at night when she squinted her one not so swollen eye open. She saw what looked like vehicle headlights shining through the trees. She doesn't remember all the details, but she believed a man in a truck found her lying there in the woods. He helped her into his truck and was going to take her to the hospital. She begged him not to. She asked him to bring her to my co-worker friend's house.

After negotiating through a third party over the phone like a hostage exchange, I went to retrieve my little Punkin. All battered and bruised with her new short orange butch haircut. Back to the house we drove to pack what was left of her bedroom belongings. While Marie was on the run, I went through her CDs with a hammer and trash bag. No more of that kind of music in my house. I pitched all her stuffed animals including her little stuffed lambie that played "You

Are My Sunshine". I would wind up that key and sing to her every night before bed when she was little. I may have gone too far with throwing away reminders of those memories, but I was angry, I was scared, and I didn't know if I was ever going to see her again.

traded her car to a co-worker friend for his help painting the house. He and his wife had a whole tribe of kids and would eventually pass that Hooptie down through every one of them. I ceremoniously cut up Marie's driver's license, as if it mattered, since she would certainly figure out a way to get a new one. I truly believed we would be making a fresh start with earning back perks and privileges.

At this point Marie's life is half over:

As all this drama was occurring, I was once again caught up in the BRAC Base Realignment and Closure process for closing government facilities and consolidating functions at other government facilities. I was in the process of selling the house in preparation for another BRAC move. So screw that school, that town, and their bullies. Once again, we were on the road to a fresh start with all the hopes and promises of a better future.

This time we were off to Fort Monmouth, New Jersey where I was informed during the pre-move seminar that the school was more integrated with diverse military and government kids who tended to look out for each other. When making temporary living arrangements during the house hunting phase, my only request was we not stay at a Comfort Inn.

Marie's hair was growing out by now and she kept the new color only a more toned-down shade of orange.

One thing about Marie, she was inclined to have one or two very close friends that she trusted. She had a lot of BFF photos among her new collection of refreshed phot albums. Her friends meant a lot to Marie. They would either be staying at our house for a few days or at their house. They were so much alike they were often thought of as sisters. It was so nice that her friends came from military families.

When the last place I worked closed due to BRAC, the woman that was at the house when the police showed up for the Domestic violence call, was going to lose her job. I invited her to move along with us and take the position offered to her at the new location. It was the least I could do. She was younger than me and sort of got along with Marie. She had been adopted as a baby from one of those countries above the Arctic Circle by a couple in Virginia. She had a bit of teenage history herself. To include a stint in rehab.

Even in her new High School. Marie tended to take on the cliques and bullies that preyed on the loners or less popular kids. Now that she thought of herself as an expert, she was once again labeled a troublemaker by certain teachers. One teacher said that Marie predictably wasn't going to be very successful in life. We had to fight with that teacher and the principals just to get her to the front of the classroom. This teacher would bring a lawyer to parent teacher conferences just for us.

Parent teacher conferences were conducted in the gymnasium where parents stood in line in front of tables waiting their turn to sit next to the table and chat with the teacher. Perhaps there had been a previous incident, and they didn't want teachers and parents to be alone in a classroom. With the teacher, the Lawyer and the Principal present, it was explained to me that other kids in class would be denied the right to an education if the teacher had to put Marie in the front of the room and move the smart kids to the back of the room.

Having been the night custodian of both Middle and High School, I mentioned that I had dust mopped many a classroom with various configurations to accommodate all students in the classroom. Thus, ensuring that every student has an equal right to an education. I said, For example, "the Horseshoe arrangement." I also mentioned that I spoke to other teachers who told me they learn many of these contemporary ideas by attending teacher in-service seminars. I was then informed that this teacher had 25 years of experience and knew what was best for her classroom without attending any seminars. What would you have said next?

This time we had the student counselor who supported Marie but was afraid to confront the administration and lose his job over one student. Marie also had a couple teachers who thought she was the greatest kid ever.

I did, however, recognize that Marie became very interested in art and theater. Her drawings were beautiful, and she wrote poetry all the time. Some of it was outstanding. Perhaps she was developing a less aggressive method of dealing with her anger and frustration.

Marie received a Leadership award from her performing arts teachers. She had Marie incorporate some country dance steps into the choreography for their school performances. How do you get Marie interested in school? Let her help teach the other kids. Especially the kids in the back of the classroom. I was becoming hopeful that Marie would eventually graduate from High School.

Marie was very athletic. She did find the time to play softball on the High School varsity team. She started at second base but could also pitch, which she did in her summer league. Occasionally, I had the opportunity to share some of my expertise as an assistant coach. They were the misfits of the league, of course. Like the Bad News Bears. I would have the base runners keep going. The other team would see them still running and start throwing the ball around in a panic. I learned that coaching peewee baseball. It was possible to score double digits runs in one inning.

Marie and her BFF also participated in the High School color guard. Kind of a surprise since cheerleaders and color guard could tend to be a bit cliquey. Thankfully her BFF was also in the color guard. They spent hours together practicing routines and creating some routines of their own.

Marie was a Junior in High school by the time I was re-married. Yes, to the young lady that moved with us to New Jersey. Marie had a blast helping with the planning, decorating the hall, and doing the bride's hair and makeup. We had a Country Cowboy wedding with hats boots and lots of country dancing. I realized from our time in Georgia how important it is to have loving and caring friends that trust each other.

Speaking of trust. Now that we had two vehicles, Marie was given the privilege to drive one of the vehicles to school. The rules were simple, drive directly to school and home unless we gave her permission. No one else rides with her unless we give her permission. It took about two weeks before we got the call that Marie was in an accident and someone else was driving. Luckily, once again, it was the other driver's fault. Marie let her friend drive and they totaled the car. Luckily It was the other driver's fault. Marie stopped at an intersection to allow an emergency vehicle with its flashing lights and siren on to pass in front of them. A car crashed into them from behind.

You may be asking how she got her license in the first place, since I told her no driver's license when we got to New Jersey. She was able to circumvent the driver's license restriction I imposed on her when we moved to New Jersey by getting to know a young man, who happened to be a rookie police officer assigned to the DMV, so smart.

Getting Marie to Wisconsin and Michigan to spend time with my actual family was challenging over the years. We seemed to be moving all the time and could never get closer than 800 miles from any members of my family. I tried to get her to see and experience family whenever the opportunity presented itself. I took her to Wisconsin on time and had her stay at my sister's dairy farm. Marie had two cousins there that were her age. She got to experience some fresh dairy air and helped deliver a calf that was being born in the barn. I brought her to my class reunion one time. She learned quickly from my old classmates that I wasn't the saint I projected when one called me Weed hopper. Her face lit up as she looked me right in the eye and said, "you are so busted". She asked why they called me weed hopper. I simply explained because Grasshopper had already been taken in the TV show Kung Fu.

That following summer we all went to Arnold, Michigan for a family reunion on my mother's side. While at the family reunion, Marie and her cousins decided to pitch a tent and camp in the field about a hundred yards behind the house. Besides being located nearly in the middle of Upper Peninsula Michigan, Arnold is literally in the middle of nowhere. I mentioned that I remember when I was growing up, we would go back there to the family dump to see the Black bears. They started out bravely and had fun trying to set up their tent. But when it started raining and got a little dark, they decided to come back to the house and sleep in the big open bedroom above the garage where my cousins slept when they were growing up. They had lots of kids and required frequent expansion to accommodate and separate the boys and girls. The girls had bedrooms and the boys had barracks.

The next day we all huddled under the big, rented party tent. There was food, drinks and a nice warm fire. My sister and brother-in-law had a band and were going to have a tent dance later that evening. That was the first time Marie complained of a severe headache. It was almost emergency room worthy, but the closest medicine man was fifty miles away. We were in the middle of Yooper land.

That was the first sign, other than when I asked her if she was brain damaged, that Marie might have serious brain issues. We didn't consider it that serious at the time because she had slept above the garage where the kerosene heater was just down below her on the ground floor. We thought it was possibly carbon monoxide. She took some Excedrin Migraine and that was the end of that. From that day on Marie suffered in silence, taking aspirin and other off-the-shelf migraine medication. Although now that I remember, it was my mother's family that was stricken with more than one type of cancer to include the first of my uncles to die from cancer, had brain cancer.

Just because we moved away from the trouble in Virginia by no means meant that old habits didn't die. Marie just got better at not getting caught, until. We had a different house with no direct access to the outside from her bedroom, however it was not inescapable. I received a call at 3:00 A.M. from the police station. They requested that I come and pick up one each Lindsy Marie from the Red Bank, New Jersey police station. She had been charged with being out after curfew. I said that's impossible, she is home in bed. I made a quick check thinking I was right for once. Nope, at least I knew where she was this time.

So, Marie had this friend, which once again impaired her judgement. They decided to sneak Marie out and go get a late-night snack at the old classic Diner in Red Bank. Which happened to be right next to the Red Bank police station. One diligent police officer, just getting off shift, noticed the registration was expired on one of the cars. He ran the plates and discovered there was a warrant for the registered owner. Who just happened to be Marie's friend. So, they proceeded to arrest the driver, leaving Marie without an adult to accompany her after curfew. The first words out of my mouth were, "can you keep her there?" I got a rather stern, no we can't.

Once again, I put on clean underwear, got dressed, and off I went. There wasn't any traffic. When I arrived, there was Marie's adult friend all dressed in an orange jumpsuit on her way to county jail. I glanced over at the desk and thought it was interesting that they were writing up the report on an old key typewriter. I thought of the Barney Miller show. I looked over at Marie who was sitting on a wooden bench against the wall. All I said was, let's go. She didn't even complain when I woke her up to catch the school bus. Perhaps she saw a good old-fashioned spanking in that cloud above her head.

Marie's last year of High School. When Marie turned eighteen, she faced some harsh reality. She had about four months left before she would graduate. She knew I wasn't going to let her just keep living with me. She surely knew I wasn't going to continue supporting the lifestyle to which she had become accustomed. Although she did have a somewhat normal school year with all the activities. She had a very nice Prom that year with all the trimmings.

It was time we had a serious discussion about her future. Still not getting it, I insisted on offering her what I thought was the best opportunity. Join the military. It worked for me when I had a wife, a baby, a seasonal job as a framing carpenter and no health insurance. She agreed and we signed her up for delayed enlistment into the United States Air Force. She scored very high on the aptitude test in career fields oriented toward medical or social work. Imagine that? someone who fought with people most of her life best suited to helping people that were struggling with their own difficult issues. She would have her diploma and a career that would train and support her potentially for the next 20 years. I felt a surge of pride and accomplishment.

Well, as you may have surmised, she wasn't having that. What was I thinking? Marie, in true Marie fashion, quit high school three months before she was going to graduate to avoid being enlisted in the Air Force. The Air Force requires a High School diploma. The United States Air Force was as pissed off as I was. She said it was because she wanted to be a Crew Chief. Who the hell gave her that idea? That is when I had enough. I told her she had to move out on her own. She was 18 now and knew everything. As often as I heard my father say, "If you think you have somewhere better to be, you better get there before it closes".

She had friends who quit school earlier that year. They had an apartment. One of them even had a job. Marie's friend, whom I called Big Bird, because she was very tall and her legs angled in at the knees and out at her feet, along with two guys, invited her to stay with them. She could stay as long as she paid her share of the rent on time every month. So, Marie and her cat KC moved in with the three of them. Lock stock and litter box. Two professional women and a cat shared one room, and two guys who seemed to never leave the apartment shared the other room.

I was then free to move about the country. When my wife, Marie's new stepmom, and I were offered a one-year assignment in Huntsville, Alabama, we packed our stuff into a friend's garage and off we went. Leaving Marie behind to prosper and experience the wonders of adulthood with her faithful and trusting friends. We did not communicate for the next nine months.

Since Marie was now on her own, she needed a car. I started her off on her independent journey with her own 1984 Honda Prelude. That car wouldn't make it ten miles without her having to stop and reconnect the vacuum hose to get it running again. It was a simple fix. I was sure Marie would figure out that a new hose or a little electrical tape around the connection would do the trick. I told her when she got her license that her first car would be commensurate with her GPA upon graduation from High school. She got what she earned without even graduating.

With the Air Force out of the question, Marie found work in a Northern New Jersey strip club. She worked as a bartender and earned a little more in tips selling shots as the walk around Shot Girl. Occasionally the club would feature Barmaid Rama Night. Where the bartenders and shot girls could get up on stage and perform. Marie said she made more money that night than any night tending bar. You can imagine how proud I was of my little Punkin.

She did make a lot of money though. She always stuck up for the dancers when clients would get unruly. Some of the girls were Russian. Apparently, there was some kind of agreement between the two management factions allowing interns from Russia to work alongside the American girls. As Marie explained the intricacies of strip clubbing in New Jersey to me. Sometimes her sticking up for the dancers could get dangerous and was frowned upon by the management. No kidding.

Marie also made some very interesting friends while working in such a high-class establishment. Like her bouncer friends that drove Corvettes and wore little gold fertility horn necklaces. I am guessing it was in her best interest to have someone sticking up for her at the same time she was sticking up for others. That's when Marie became a real Jersey Girl. She spent much of her free time at the Jersey Shore. Marie was fearless.

I spent the next nine months in Alabama. We were working on the next BRAC project for the Command we worked under in New Jersey. We were making friends. We spent many nights playing cards and enjoying hanging out with the neighbors across the street, we were playing a lot of golf, we went to Nashville. We were just enjoying life. We experienced a few tornadoes and tried to get on TV to say, "it sounded like a freight train".

This is not my story, so back to Marie. Upon our return to New Jersey nine months later. We bought into a condo complex and retrieved our furniture from my friend's garage. It was on the ground floor and had a nice big basement. We turned the basement into a Recreational room with a large screen TV. No room for renters.

Shortly after settling in, Marie called me in tears asking to come back home. I didn't see that coming, or did I? I said "one question" have you passed your GED? She said no but she wanted me to come to her work so we could talk. So, there I was, sitting at the bar in a New Jersey strip club. Marie asked me for a $20.00 bill and handed me a stack of ones. She said she would be on break in a few, and not to spend it all in one place. The girl dancing on the bar was Marie's friend whom she would later bring home for dinner.

I wasn't going to let her move back in with us, period. She hadn't yet passed her GED. She said she was trying to move out of her apartment, but her roommates wouldn't let her. She got stuck paying all the utilities and her rent was the only rent being paid on time. She was what kept them from being evicted. When she said she was afraid for her cat I knew I had to get her out of there.

Her mother must have missed her because our discussion included Marie staying with me until her mother could fly there, and they could drive the rental truck back to Atlanta. That's how her mother delivered her to me when Marie was twelve. This could be a little payback and maybe Marie would at least appreciate what I tried to do for her all those years.

So, we rented a Ryder truck and pulled up at the apartment. Marie's bouncer friends from the strip club pulled up to the apartment in their Corvette and parked it right next to the truck. A couple tan bodybuilding type Italian horn wearing Jersey talking well-groomed young men had no trouble persuading Marie's roommates to let her leave. They helped us pack up her belongings and load them, and KC into a rental truck. It was the first time I got to see what Marie's apartment looked like. I don't know how she lived like that for that long. It must have been torture. Good.

Her mother flew to New Jersey. We picked her up at Newark Airport and we took her to the condo. She didn't even want to spend the night leaving the next morning. Not like we didn't have room. In the truck they climbed with KC and the litter box. Back to Atlanta they headed down the Turnpike. Towing her Honda behind them on a car carrier trailer. Marie certainly didn't need any more wear and tear on those tires.

While on their way south down Interstate 95, they discussed how things would be and the wonderful opportunity that was being offered to Marie. They eventually ran out of nice things to say to each other. Suddenly her mother started laying down the law. Getting a Job, curfew, household chores, and all the expectations her mother had for their renewed relationship. Marie was a captive audience and had no choice but to listen and agree.

Once she was back in Atlanta, the first thing Marie did was take her GED test. She passed with flying colors. She came close to scoring 100%. That would definitely help her get a better job. Unfortunately, staying with her mother lasted only a couple months before, according to Marie, she broke the 10:00 curfew one Saturday night and was told to move out. I guess her mother was serious about the rule of law in her house. Marie lasted longer than I thought. I was sure she would be back in New Jersey hustling tips, or worse. Lesson learned.

Marie went back to Kennesaw and moved in with her grandparents, at her mother's extreme displeasure. Marie's grandparents may have broken the law as well. While living with her mother she found a job working with children in a Montessori school. She loved that job, except her Honda kept breaking down on the I-285 Atlanta Beltway because of that damn vacuum hose. I believe her Papa finally taped it together. I can't believe after all I taught her that she didn't figure out how to fix that hose. I am sure she kept meaning to get some electrical tape one day.

Working with those kids was a great job for Marie. She really did love children, and she was very good as a teacher. Not long after moving in with her grandparents, Marie quit the Montessori job and worked at different Bars and restaurants closer to where she was living. Including my favorite, the Waffle House right off I-285. I bet she applied there one day when her car broke down.

During the time Marie was settling into her independent life, I moved with my wife to a new condo complex that was just opening. We decided after all our friends were getting divorced, there was no more dancing, and there was no longer a Country Radio station in New York City, that we would get a very amiable divorce. Quite Frankly, it was the day the music died. She moved on to Rock and Roll. Our wedding song was by Neil McCoy, "Tell me you love me for a million years, and if it don't work out, we can just say good bye".

I was also thinking about going to Iraq for six months and she was perfectly ok with staying in the condo while I was gone. Not long after I left for Iraq, she found a new love interest and was very happy. I was happy for her. She deserved it. My life was soon to be headed in a very dark direction. She certainly didn't deserve to be so young, having to deal with the journey Marie and I were headed toward.

I am not sure what made Marie get into playing billiards. Maybe it was her freedom to go out at night after she moved in with her grandparents. Maybe it was her stint in the Strip club, she started going to a pool hall which became her social life. Her favorite game was nine-ball. She was good at it. She had her own cue stick, cue stick carrying case, even a trophy or two.

The best I can surmise from events that followed; Marie found a young lady living in a car behind the pool hall. I am not sure if she knew this girl in a previous life, or they just met for the first time. Marie apparently got to know her and trusted her. She offered the spare bedroom in her apartment to this young lady. Marie allowed her to live there for free while she got her life together and finished her education. I don't know if free is the right word if you know what it is like to live with Marie.

That young lady still calls me Dad today. All grown up, with a nurse's assistant certification from the University of Georgia and two kids of her own. Those two became nine-ball tournament pool shooting BFF Sisters. Marie and Missy traveled around the Southeast to play nine-ball pool tournaments. Missy has more stories about Marie, and after living with Marie, probably knew Marie better than anyone else.

Now that Marie was on her own with a career, it wasn't long before I came back into Marie's life. I would spend the major holidays with Marie and Missy. I would try to do something special with them every August for Marie's Birthday. They were even more like sisters by this time. No matter what we did, it was with the two of them together.

During one of my vacations, I took the two of them to Wal-Mart and gave them each a shopping cart. I told them to fill it up with things they need and maybe a couple things they want. I think Marie was a little jealous, but I was happy for the two of them to be and act like sisters.

They Had very specific places they went to eat. I took them to a place of my choosing one time and one time only. Marie ordered the beef tips. After she sent them back twice and said they taste like doodoo, the chef was so pissed off, he came out of the kitchen all red faced with a meat cleaver.

It was a constant challenge to make Marie happy. Every vacation was more like going to work. Going back to work was more like a vacation after a vacation with Marie. I helped her buy a new car and she picked out a Ford Focus hatchback. Just her luck a tree branch fell on it during a storm which dented the roof and broke the windshield. Other than that incident, she took really good care of that car. I'm sure it was the appreciation she developed from her previous experience with her Honda Prelude.

After a couple years, and against Missy's advice, to my shock and surprise, Marie left Atlanta, drove to Seattle Washington in her new Ford Focus and got married to an Air Force C-17 Crew Chief. Which is the job Marie really wanted when she enlisted in the Air Force years earlier.

She moved to Seattle leaving Missy behind to fend for herself. There is no rhyme or reason why Marie had to get married to that person at that time. It was what she wanted to do. Missy and I did not even attend her wedding. Missy warned Marie that this guy had anger issues. What a shocker that was.

By the following Christmas Marie called me in distress. It was their first Christmas. He was not home, there were no presents other than the one crystal Newlywed ornament I sent her. She had no money, no food in the house, and she had no idea who to go to, or where to go. I had never met this young Airman, so I didn't understand what happened. I didn't like him. I had enough time in the military to know that the only way to get out of staying in the barracks in some Air Force Bases was to get married. Since his friends were at Marie's house more than they were in the barracks, I sort of got the idea. On New Years Day I was flying from Newark and landing at Seattle Tacoma Airport where Marie and her cat picked me up in her Ford Focus for the long drive back to Atlanta.

We drove through the worst snowstorm over the Pass to get into Oregon. It took us ten hours to go 300 miles. We followed tractor trailer trucks, being careful not to get a flat tire from running over their lost tire chains in the road. We got as far as Yakima on New Years Day during the worst storm recorded in Yakima. We had to try and find some tire chains, or they wouldn't let us over the next Pass. Not able to find chains we were forced to take the low road along a winding river. Every tractor trailer truck that didn't have chains went roaring past us in the opposite direction. I kept glancing down the long steep bank to the river that looked like frozen water as it flowed through the rapids. We finally got over the Pass and into Oregon. We stayed the remainder of the night in one of those quaint Oregon log cabin style motels. The next morning, we had a hot breakfast. After a short scolding by the gas station attendant for trying to pump our own gas, we were on our way. There are only two states that don't let you pump your own gas. Oregon and New Jersey.

We drove through Idaho into Utah passing though Salt Lake City.

By the time we crossed into Wyoming it was freezing cold windblown snow on the icy interstate. We stopped for a break at a Harley dealer and bought a couple T-Shirts. Then we continued to Cheyanne where we went south until we stopped for the night in Fort Collins, Colorado. We stayed at Motel 6. They left the light on for us.

The snow was falling when we woke up. We had to hurry to get on the road before it got too bad to drive without chains. Cars were sliding all over the road and off the ramps as we drove through Denver to Interstate 70.

Then it was East to Kansas where the snow changed to rain. We had a badly screeching windshield wiper for about a hundred miles before we could get a replacement blade at a truck stop. By late afternoon we were hungry and wanted to have a steak dinner. Not much open so we had a disappointing meal at a buffet style steak restaurant. Where you move through the line with a tray and tell them what steak meal you want. They cook it for you while you get your potato and salad, grab your number and go sit down to wait.

We were back on the road. When the sun went down the road turned to glare ice. We crept along with the endless line of traffic. Cars were attempting to pass and slid right into the snow filled median. We made it down the long hill into the outskirts of Kansas City. Everyone was creeping along with their passenger side tires on the gravel to keep from sliding into the car in front of them. We found a cheap motel and slept soundly that night.

The next morning, I looked out the window at the car around 5:30 AM. Oh shit, it was coated in ice at least a quarter inch thick. I tried to pour some cold water on it, chopped it, scraped it and waited an hour for the defroster to make even a small clear circle at the bottom of the windshield.

We finally got it clear, filled up with gas, grabbed some coffee and snacks and we were on the road again. Our next stop was to take our picture at the Super Man stand behind the cutout phot op. May as well enjoy the tourist stops and sights along the way.

We had a three-day drive through 10 states to talk about life and the pursuit of happiness.

We listened to the audio recording of the book Men are from Mars, Women are from Venus. I have no idea why Marie had that CD. We spent hours discussing all the statements, questions, and conclusions explained in the book. Some of it made sense to me, some of it made sense to Marie. I basically told her my opinion was that men and women are from Earth and we need to get it figured out on our own. Which we were both doing.

Marie would sit in silence for hours. I could tell she was holding back tears. She was obviously very sad that what she thought was real love didn't work out. So many lessons learned for a beautiful young lady at such a young age. She certainly lived her share of love's brutal disappointments.

To make the trip more pleasant we stopped at all the Stucky's rest stops and collected the little State magnets for the refrigerator. I still have some of those magnets on the side of the fridge. We drove through the worst snowstorm in Washington and Oregon State, the coldest night in Wyoming, more winter conditions in Colorado, and the worst ice storm in Kansas and Missouri. The remainder of the trip south out of Illinois through Nashville, Chattanooga, and on to Kennesaw went relatively smoothly.

It was the most bonding time I spent with Marie. At some point during that portion of the trip, she promised me she would get divorced and never get married again. She also promised to change her last name back to Weaver which she would not change again. All I wanted was if she ever got married again, I would be there to give her away properly. Then we didn't stop until we got to Atlanta where we camped on the floor at Nanny and Papa's house. They were my Ex-In-laws, but I really missed them. Nanny was British by birth and always had a nice hot cup of tea ready for me. A hot cup of tea with a bit of brandy is a way of letting anyone know that everything will be all right.

Marie and Missy were back together. After a short recovery, Marie went back to work. She worked at a couple of different places until she ultimately landed a position in the management office at an apartment complex. I believe they gave her an apartment, or at least one to rent at a discount. She liked having a place to live on her own. She was very good at her job. She would show apartments, interview clients, manage the cleaning and custodial staff, and complete the monthly financial reports. Most importantly, she was going to qualify for health insurance if she could just stay in one place long enough.

Missy moved in with Marie. She continued her studies and continued to help Marie with laundry, cooking and cleaning. The two of them played pool in tournaments. They started hanging out at the country bar, going to concerts and frequenting their favorite exclusive eating establishments. Our holiday and Birthday visits continued for another year until New Years Eve 2005 just before I left for Iraq. We spent that New Years Eve together at Cowboys, the classy country dance and concert venue in Kennesaw. We danced, drank and were Merry in our Country cowboy get up and boots.

I flew back to New Jersey and a couple weeks later I headed to pre-deployment training at Ft. Bliss, TX.

One of the toughest phone calls we had was just before I boarded the plane headed to Kuwait, then on to Baghdad. We weren't sure if we would ever see each other again. I promised to call her whenever I could, and she promised to be good. That phone was a little damp from tears after all the calls made that night, including mine.

I spent the next six months on the logistics staff of the Multi-National Security Transition Command-Iraq. Under the command of Major General Petraeus. Our mission included equipping and training the Iraqi army and police. I spent some of my time contracting for, and driving, a South African designed armored truck through the streets of Baghdad patrolling police stations and escorting officials around the Baghdad area.

I volunteered to teach dance lessons in the Presidential Palace. My class included the Army doctors and nurses of the 86th Combat Support Hospital. They enjoyed the time to unwind. I taught country and swing dancing on Saturday nights. I especially enjoyed when the Coalition troops from places like Norway or Australia would show up. What an adventure.

Every night back in my hooch I counted and crossed through the day on my wall calendar. We waited for mail call every afternoon. I made it my responsibility to get the mail for my office and find out why, when it didn't show up. Mail call meant time to take a break from the long day, it was almost over. It was a very lonely six months. I did not receive one letter from any of my family the whole time I was in Iraq. Maybe I forgot to tell them.

People were arriving and people were leaving. Some days were endless boredom. Driving in and around Baghdad made for a long day but far from boring. Imagine yourself driving through towns and cities knowing that someone was trying to kill you. Back to Marie's story.

While I was in Iraq, Marie proceeded slowly with her divorce. I believe it was because her estranged husband was not willing to give up their escape from the barracks into free on-base housing, where he and his friends took up residence, allegedly.

I would get updates occasionally, but we had difficulty communicating across the world. When we did get to call, we talked about what we would do for her next Birthday when I got back home to New Jersey. I would call my office and they would patch me through to an outside phone line to Marie's phone number. Some people will have no idea what that means.

When I finally did get back to New Jersey, the two girls and I followed through on our plan to take the train into New York City, see a play on not necessarily Broadway, and check out the night life afterwards. Marie was very good in her high school drama class and really loved New York City.

I had a friend with a pool that lived a couple miles from my house. The girls stayed with her while I was at work. I would only work half a day. Not like they got out of bed before 11:00. They would be floating in the pool or soaking in the hot tub when I got there. I brought Marie and Missy a couple camouflage floppy hats back from Iraq. They wore those things every day at the pool.

The trip into NYC had its challenges. The off-Broadway show we attended was a mock wedding play called "Tony and Tina's Wedding". The audience was all members of the mock Mafia family. It was quite entertaining. The actors paid a lot of attention to Marie and Missy. I was in the Bathroom scene when a couple of the actors came into the bathroom.

After the show Marie and Missy hit the town. I was too anxious and protective for their safety, just getting back from Iraq. There was no way I could hang out with Marie in New York City at night. Especially taking the kinds of chances she took and being in that part of the city.

I had to just let her go and enjoy the night in the city that never sleeps. I was back in the room waiting to hear them come in so I could get to sleep. The next morning it was back on the train to Jersey. Marie blew out her candles and then it was back to Atlanta for Marie and Missy after a somewhat successful 26th Birthday.

Marie still hadn't finished her divorce and needed some more help. She tried to get back some personal items which were eventually returned all broken. I guess you just can't have nice things and get through a divorce. We kept working through the process of getting paperwork passed back and forth. She had most of what she wanted. She had her cat and her car. That was all she needed except to get her name changed back to her maiden name.

After Iraq I was assigned to the Counter Improvised Explosive Device (IED) program for the Army. Basically, radio jamming the roadside bombs in Iraq and Afghanistan. It was a 24 hour /7 day a week job. I had almost no time for anything. I'd get home late, answer emails in the middle of the night, and be back at work early in the morning.

Marie acquired her certification for managing apartments and was promoted to assistant manager at her new complex. Marie had a boyfriend, and Missy had a boyfriend. Both young men were prior military. One a Marine and one a Sniper in Bosnia. They were both gentlemen and seemed to be respectful of the girls. Together they were doing well except for the usual petty drama that surrounded Marie at work and play. Marie had her way of doing things. Like folding towels, washing dishes, and any critique of how Missy did housework.

After three months on the job Marie qualified for company sponsored health care which was always a milestone for her to achieve. She was socially engaged in company business, and various social events. She still had to deal with the constant headaches. Her friends all watched her chew extra strength Excedrin Migraine like candy. Every day was a challenge for her and the people who loved her watched as she became very predictably unpredictable.

Marie and Missy became amateur tournament pool players and would also frequent their favorite country bar and concert venue in Kennesaw called Cowboys. They got to know the owner, the staff, and the band. They attended several concerts evidenced by the number of autographed signs and photographs in her and Missy's apartment.

By October 2005 Marie was experiencing more severe headaches. Her boyfriend was getting frustrated with Marie avoiding a visit to the doctor to get it checked out. Not sure how but he finally convinced her to get a doctor to check her out so she could get stronger prescription medication. She went for a few tests which were now covered by her insurance. The doctor had her do a simple balance test and

Marie faltered just slightly. Based on that slight balance issue, the doctor scheduled her for an immediate CT scan. Marie was told to go ahead and leave. The doctor would have to wait for the results. She promised to call Marie as soon as they received them.

Later that afternoon, Marie was attending one of the company outdoor social functions. They were cooking out, having a few drinks, and playing volleyball. The phone rang in the office and the attendant yelled to Marie that the call was for her. So right in the middle of a work social function Marie receives a somewhat panicked phone call from her doctor's office. The Doctor explained that Marie needed to make an appointment with a neurologist right away. She told Marie over the phone that the CT scan identified a mass in her brain, and they needed to another scan with contrast. Marie fainted on the spot.

If you ever wondered how many people are connected to you in life, something like this will certainly let you know. Talk about a fast-moving train. I can't even remember the details. After an MRI with contrast, it was immediately scheduling the biopsy surgery. I flew to Atlanta to be with Marie for the surgery on her brain. We gathered with some of her friends and watched the Packers lose a very close game the day before.

On that note it was time to get her affairs in order so to speak. The first thing on her list was to get her divorce over with. Then it was time to get her Last Will and Testament done to make sure her soon to be ex didn't get anything. Marie's boyfriend's mother worked for a lawyer so the Will was easy. She divided her life insurance policy and all her belongings equally between her mother and me. She also asked in her Will that she receive a Christian like burial.

The biopsy surgery was significant. We convinced the neurosurgeon not to shave her head. They stuck her head on spikes that left holes big enough to require stitches. They opened a dime sized hole in her skull. A needle probe was inserted through her brain into the tumor. I was on the phone to my family letting them know the play by play. Nanny Papa, Marie's mother, her husband, Sissy, Marie's boyfriend, I all waited anxiously. After the surgery we waited for Marie to recover and of course the results. It all went so fast and with such a sense of urgency, I believe Marie knew the answer but didn't want to accept the real answer. How long?

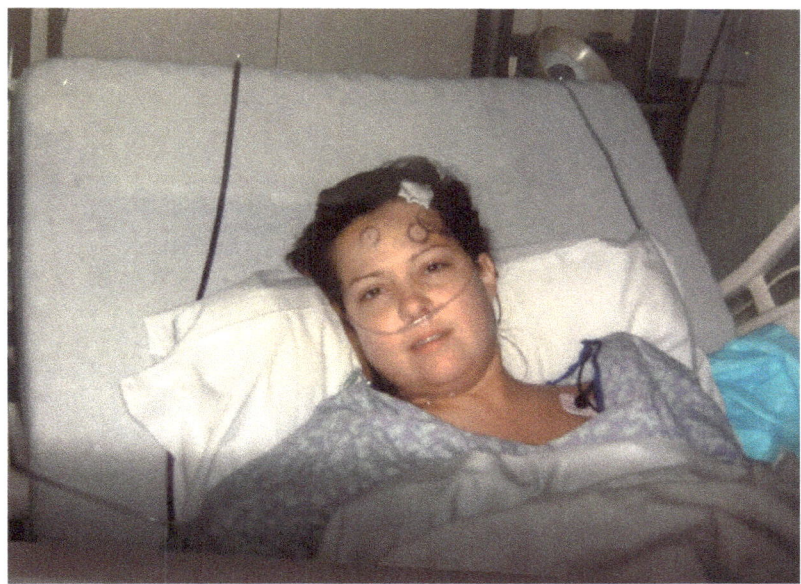

I scheduled my family sick Leave called FMLA for the rigorous six-week chemo and radiation schedule that was about to begin. I headed back home to Jersey thinking Holy crap my daughter has an incurable cancer with only one and a half to three years to live. Thanksgiving and Christmas are right around the corner.

Every day Marie drove herself to the oncology department at North Hospital. She had a pass to park close to the door in the spaces reserved for radiation patients. They greeted her in the office, and she waited patiently for her turn. They made a hard plastic mesh mask that fit over her face and bolted to a table to keep her head still. There she lay on a large table. Her head was bolted down while a very large machine rotated around her head. It would stop at different angles making noises as it sent damaging radiation energy in one side of her brain and out the other. Marie said she could see green light as the rays hit her optic nerve.

The other part of her treatment was chemo. Marie had to drive all the way across Atlanta to the oncologist since she had insurance with an HMO. She was to take a drug call Temodar. It was only experimental for brain cancer. Brain cancer is about 5% of the cancer population so they don't get all the money like breast cancer. Every patient is an experiment. Marie's oncologist explained to her that when people come to see him there are no more options. I think that is when Marie decided she would not lose this battle. At the age of 26 Marie told me she would for sure see her 30th Birthday.

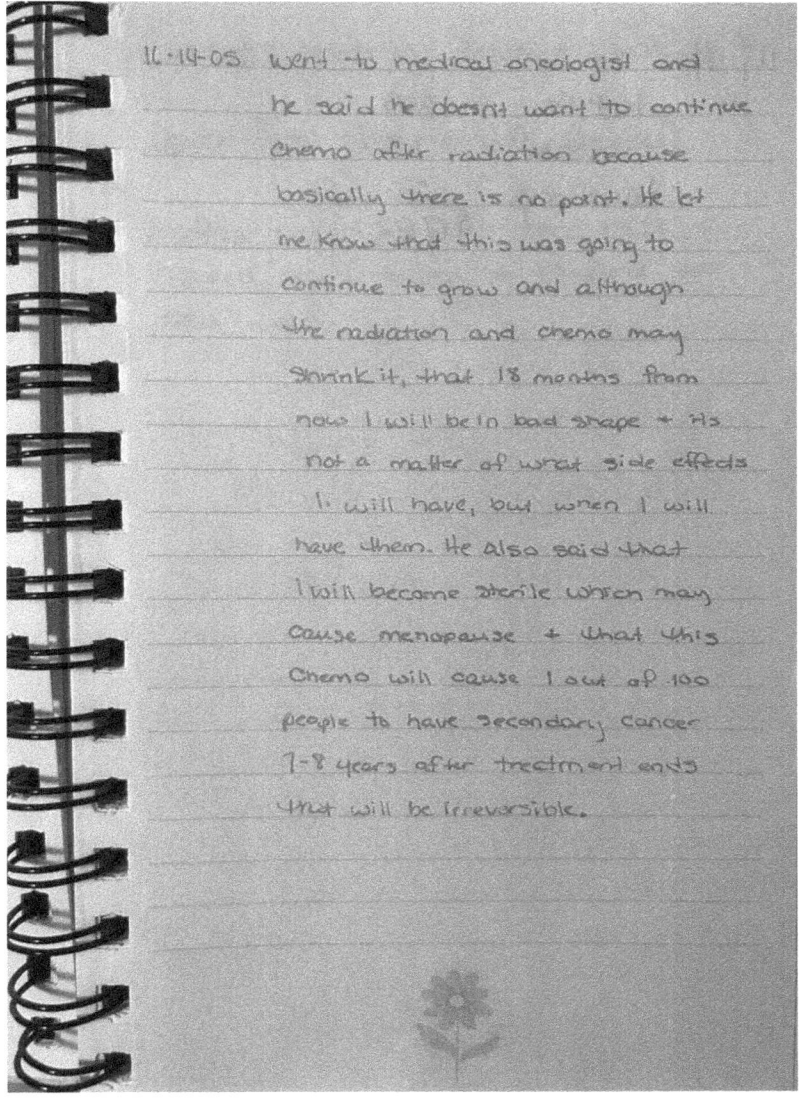

11-14-05 Went to medical oncologist and
he said he doesn't want to continue
chemo after radiation because
basically there is no point. He let
me know that this was going to
continue to grow and although
the radiation and chemo may
shrink it, that 18 months from
now I will be in bad shape + its
not a matter of what side effects
I will have, but when I will
have them. He also said that
I will become sterile which may
cause menopause + that this
chemo will cause 1 out of 100
people to have secondary cancer
7-8 years after treatment ends
that will be irreversible.

We tried to come up with a normal way to celebrate the
holidays that year. I had a timeshare in the Grand Caymans.
I banked the week and scheduled a week in Myrtle Beach
because Grandpa and Jean would be there. Marie would

have one more week of treatment, so we got them to let her take that week off between Christmas and New Years. She would have to go back for one more week after New Years.

We had a less than Grand Cayman style timeshare that slept six less than comfortably. There was even a bit of mold in the bathroom. Sissy and Jeremy drove from Atlanta, Lori flew in from Denver, I flew from New Jersey, and Judy and Bobby came from Green Bay. I flew Marie to Myrtle Beach from Atlanta as she was too beaten up from her treatments to ride in the car. Marie was so uncomfortable every minute. She was having hot flashes, her head hurt, she had no hair, and her wig was hot and itchy.

We dragged her from show to show, the alligator farm, to the aquarium, House of Blues, and back to more Christmas shows. Her patience was courageous and admirable. She got upset over taking her picture. She felt fat and ugly. She was taking steroids that left her face full of cists. Every night she would get dressed, put on her makeup to cover the blemishes, fix her wig and go out as if nothing were wrong with her.

We all have personal stories of that week with Marie. We were all seeing Marie at her absolute worst, yet she laughed at the comedy show and sat through the Christmas shows. We danced at the Beach Wagon while my sister and brother-in-law played with the band. That night dancing with Marie is engrained in my heart forever. Everyone who was there will never forget it. After all the shows and all the pictures, we went back to our homes.

Marie went back to North Hospital for the last week of her radiation treatments. Her face was so swollen that her plastic mask left mesh marks on her face. Her chemo oncologist had been reluctant to prescribe her more than a week's worth of pills during the six weeks in case she didn't make it that long. She had to drive to the other side of Atlanta every week to get her prescription renewed. The HMO would lose money if they wasted the pill that couldn't be returned. Marie promised that no matter what, she would never go through radiation and chemo again.

After her treatments Marie tried to get back to living. She returned to work after taking time off the entire month of January to recover. While she was gone a temp hire took her place and became quite good friends with the Manager. The accounting books were left unattended for the two months Marie was out. That gave her the month of February to catch up. Because February is such a short month, she wasn't quite able to get it done. The manager wrote up Marie for all the unfinished accounts then wrote up Marie for not being able to do her job. The write-up was quite extensive and listed several shortfalls in Marie's performance. Marie was very upset. They sent her to the corporate office for basically termination counseling. They negotiated either letting her go or taking a lesser position so the Temp hire could take her job. Marie was now absolutely devastated. She wanted to file a discrimination lawsuit.

I had a better idea. Filing discrimination might get her job back with the same people. I asked for the letter. Since Marie worked long enough for medical insurance, she also had disability insurance. With a letter signed by everyone in her corporation she had her ticket to free money. Long term disability really pissed off her minority counterparts. Now all we had to do was get her Social Security benefits which would put her on a fixed income for the rest of her life. I began the process and hired an attorney to get the social security part going. I just wanted her to be able to live anywhere she wanted and have enough money to live on. She stayed in the apartment for the duration of her lease. She picked up another stray cat so now she had two pets in her menagerie.

Marie finally got her maiden name back. She was officially divorced and promised again never to change her name. We set up a joint checking account in case she needed help with her finances, or I needed access to her estate. No more working for Marie. She could now start working on her bucket list. Marie was free to go wherever she wanted and live the rest of her life doing what she wanted to do. I had been traveling all over the world so I was thinking I could get Marie out to see some of it. I reluctantly had to settle for what she wanted to do.

Marie moved in with her boyfriend at his grandmother's house. Missy moved in with her boyfriend at his parent's house. Then they got a dog. Marie decided that now she wanted to spend her time being a homebody with her animals instead of seeing the world. Marie was destined to be a pet owner and the pets would pretty much determine how her life would be spent. She still had KC the cat from when she was seven years old. Marie now had three pets in her menagerie.

Marie was trying, but for whatever reason she wasn't happy in Atlanta. I thought it was time for her to get more acquainted with her Weaver family heritage, so we discussed moving her to Green Bay. At the time, I was hoping one day to return to Green Bay after I retired. I thought maybe we could find the right house for both of us. She would live in it for as long as she could then I would rent it out until I retired.

We moved Marie to Green Bay in 2006. I set it up so she and her grandpa could go house hunting together. She looked at several houses on the West side of town where the relatives all live. After her house hunting trip with Grandpa, she decided to buy an old house on the East side where she and her Army sniper moved in with KC John Wayne and Nellie the dog. Nobody on the west side likes to cross the river to the east side but that is where she decided to live. I guess there are reasons for everything. Then she got another dog. A part Mastiff Marmaduke looking thing she named Sebastian. Now there were four animals in her menagerie.

I sort of stepped in for her 27th Birthday and decided to work on her bucket list with her. I planned a trip to one of the nicest resorts in the Dominican Republic. Marie and I met in Atlanta and together we flew to Punta Cana in the Dominican Republic. It was a tropical paradise amidst a poverty stricken third world country. The Dominican shares half an Island with Haiti. Hidden behind very high fences away from the locals, we enjoyed a week of lounging at the pool, fine dining, Spa treatments, evening shows, adventure journeys to wild animal parks, snorkeling, shopping, dancing every night in the lounge, and a four-course dinner at the most exclusive restaurant where the Clintons allegedly dined on their vacation.

One bucket list item was for Marie to pet a white tiger. She was always very connected to white tigers. The white tiger was her totem so to speak. We also swam with Sea lions. It was like swimming with dolphins in the Caymans, only with the cutest little sea lion at the Dominican version. We all got our pictures taken, sitting next to the sea lion, getting a kiss on the cheek. The little sea lion settled next to Marie and kissed her on the head, right on her tumor. Marie's adventure tour included wrapping a Python around her neck, holding an Iguana, and taking a picture of me with two baby parrots sitting on my head.

When we got back from the Dominican Marie got to spend time with her mother in Atlanta before returning to Green Bay.

Back in Green Bay Life went on. Marie was learning the complexities of family relationships and obligations. She tried to keep up with everyone. She had difficulty traveling to the west side of town and the family had difficulty traveling to the east side. I would make trips to Green Bay for the Holidays and shuttle back and forth.

Marie and her cousin tried to keep up with each other, but her cousin had two kids and Marie had two dogs that were like her kids. I got to follow the dynamics from afar. All in all, everyone tried their best. Marie's condition brought me closer to a family I had also left behind and didn't see except for a couple of high school class reunions and a few holidays over the years.

With everyone more involved in my life, because of Marie, it was time to face the past and surface that old family secret. I am not so sure it was a secret to anyone. As far as this family was concerned bygones had been bygones for a long time. Marie's Aunt Judy presented the idea of introducing Marie to her half-brother. I suppose I need to explain. I had not tried to contact the young man since the late 80's. I sent a letter and some pictures after which his adopted father wrote telling me to stay away and never try to contact him again.

That one time was also instigated by my sister. The boy's mother and I were high school sweethearts. I went away to college on a scholarship for ski-jumping where I won the junior national championship and was about to be named to the 1976 US Ski Team. Then I came home from college.

I totally understand how having the same situation happen to her only two daughters drove a mother to revenge rather than compassion. I also understand that when a father has the same situation with two sons, it is less likely that the second son gets much sympathy. It wasn't going to be up to me.

Buying a ring and promising to do the right thing was common in those days. Especially those of us who grew up Catholic. So that is what I did. That's what my dad did. However, given the circumstances and the personalities involved, that was not an acceptable course of action for us.

I tried to prove myself worthy and searched for any job I could find. I applied at Paper Mills, I tried selling Dyna Gym exercise equipment, I tried the shipping docks at the harbor, canning companies, I couldn't even get hired at the slaughterhouse killing cows or shoveling guts into the furnace. I wasn't Union. Dad was Union. Why didn't dad get me in at the Paper Mill? Because he got my older brother in at the paper mill. My older brother apparently never thanked him for it. So, I was on my own. How is that for teaching my brother a lesson?

It wasn't going to matter what I did to make it right. With no job and no place to live I left the wedding rings behind. I went back to school with the money that was left of my school loan to get back into skiing the second semester at UNH. 1976 was going to be my last year skiing. If I didn't make it to the Olympics I was done. As luck would have it, I fell in the Olympic tryouts and missed my dream of going to the Innsbruck Olympics. My very last official international competition was at Pine Mountain in Iron Mountain Michigan, where I was born. It was the week before my high school girlfriend's son was born. My mother called me in New Hampshire the day he was born. There is more to that story.

I was able to get a job in New Hampshire working in a department store garden shop for $2.30 an hour. That is where I got to know Marie's mother. Her family took me in as a boarder until I could afford a place to live. I lived with them for a year. They had two daughters. Not a surprise that Marie's mother and I would become very close. We all worked at the department store together. When their father was about to retire from the Air Force, Marie's mother had to decide if she wanted to go with them or stay in New Hampshire with me. We agreed to wait until Marie's mother graduated with her maiden name. We got married in 1977 as her dad was retiring and they were packing up to move to Georgia.

We found a small upstairs apartment, but when the couch her parents gave us didn't fit up the stairs or through the door to the small upstairs deck, we had to tell the landlord we were moving again. We found another place a block away from our new jobs at a factory called Northern Heel. Where they manufactured heels for shoes and boots. Ater a year in New Hampshire, Marie's mother and I moved to Green Bay in 1978.

This time, my past was going to catch up with me. I ended up in court over what was considered that big mistake I made back in 1975. We lived and worked in Green Bay until just after Marie was born. After three appearances in court, due to some primary witness issues, possibly due to some inconsistencies in the original story, I was once again given the option to leave the state, move to Georgia, and stay with Nanny and Papa once again. Marie left Green Bay when her life was just beginning, and she wasn't going back there again until her life was almost over. That was my point.

Now back to Marie's opportunity to meet her half-brother. My sister was able to contact Marie's half-brother through his mother. They remained acquaintances because, after all, it's a small town. My sister asked if he was willing to meet with Marie. As expected, he was willing to meet Marie but would have nothing to do with the dead-beat teenaged father that abandoned him and his mother.

Marie was at least able to experience having a real brother, even if only for a moment. For that reason, it was not a big mistake in 1975. The drama with, and between Marie and family, in her condition, compounded by issues with her boyfriend, was overwhelming her. It was inevitable that Marie would not be able to sustain an extended family relationship with all the issues she was experiencing.

On the brighter side, there was one thing that bonded Marie with family. During her first summer living in Green Bay Marie was exposed to the Green Bay Packers. Brett Favre was her hero, and the Pack was "all that" for her. Marie loved to go to games. We were not your average season ticket holders, so we would try to find tickets at the games. Grandma, my mother, was Marie's Packer party partner. Whenever any personal situation would become anxious, someone would say "how bout those Packers?"

I never saw anyone barter for Packer tickets like Marie. She almost got a scalper to pay her to take his tickets. Sometimes the "C" card worked in her favor. One highlight of Marie's Green Bay experience was another item on her bucket list. Marie got to meet Brett Favre one day after practice. That was a very special day, and we are all grateful for having shared that moment with Marie.

During that second short summer everyone came to Green Bay to celebrate Marie's 28th Birthday. It is known as the RV trip to Michigan. Missy and her husband, they were now married, drove from Atlanta to Green Bay for the occasion. I flew from New Jersey and the woman I would spend the rest of my life with, " My Darling", flew in from Colorado to Green Bay. We all thought it was going to be great to party like Rock Stars on the road, in an RV.

We were going to drive from Green Bay to Felch, Michigan to party at the lake with my Darling's family. Our families had been friends since we were teenagers. Her brother and I grew up traveling to ski-jumping competitions together.

The activities for the week included fishing, boating, tubing, water skiing, cooking out, climbing to the top of Pine Mountain Ski-Jump so Marie could experience a bit of her Dad's history. Marie enjoyed spending time with my future Mother-in-Law, Nona, playing cards, drinking festive libations and chatting at the big round wooden table where we would all gather for meals. And of course, we couldn't pass up going to the Artesian Well in Norway, Michigan that never stops bubbling water into the fountain. People line up there every day to fill their jugs with fresh clean water.

Well, Marie's boyfriend was supposed to watch the house and the dogs that weekend for Marie. That didn't work out. So, added to the agenda, was chasing Marie's dog, Sebastian, all through the woods around the lake. Just to have Sebastian, or Marmaduke, or Bullwinkle, as we called him, return to camp on his own. He was sitting in the shade waiting for us to finish our search and get back to the party.

The RV trip started out as a great idea. It had all kinds of potential and certainly presented some interesting adventures. Along with some interesting drama. I considered it a very successful 28th Birthday for Marie. However, not to be outdone, the trip ended with me backing the RV into Marie's Ford Focus as I was pulling out of her driveway to return the RV to the dealership. I asked Missy's husband to move the car. So, he moved it right straight across from the driveway. Marie wanted to call the police and report an accident, even though I paid for the car, the RV, and the repairs. She thought if she reported the accident the insurance would cover the repairs. It was fortunate for me that the bumper on the RV was already bent from a previous adventurer. That's why they offer insurance when you rent them.

I went back to my 24/7 counter IED job in New Jersey and couldn't stop thinking about how much time Marie had left. After a very hard winter with lots of snow shoveling in Wisconsin, it was time to check off the homeowner wish on her bucket list. Marie was losing interest in Green Bay.

Just to make a difficult year a little more difficult, Marie's 21-year-old cat, KC passed away at the bottom of the stairs in Marie's Green Bay house. KC climbed down from the bed, where she spent all her time, to go looking for Marie. Marie was too weak and too tired. She didn't make it upstairs to bed that night. KC made it all the way down the stairs and died right outside the door to the living room where Marie was sleeping on the couch. I don't think Marie wanted to stay in Green Bay after that.

Marie had, however, made some very close friends while she was in Green Bay. She worked in an animal Groom shop part time. That kept her busy and gave her a social life. I guess living on the East Side, near her half-brother and her forever new friends, was the right thing to do after all. Even from the East side of town Marie was able to connect with more family than she had in the last 25 years of her life. Marie's relationship with her boyfriend began to strain and eventually they parted ways. He decided to move on and pursue a new love interest. leaving Marie all by herself with a big house and her two dogs.

After a few months, still working on that counter IED program in New Jersey, I figured out a way to get closer to Green Bay by requesting a compassionate reassignment from the Army. The closest location that my Army organization had to Green Bay was Rock Island Illinois. I called in some big favors and got orders to move to Rock Island. My boss and my organization were aware of my many trips to care for Marie.

Before I left New Jersey I also applied for a job in Colorado Springs. That's where my significant "other" lived. Bonus, it was on Marie's bucket list to see the world from the top of a mountain. If the Colorado job came available before I moved into a house in Rock Island, I would take it. I spent three months living and working, more like waiting, in Rock Island. Driving back and forth to Green Bay for all the Holidays.

Marie hosted Thanksgiving at her house that year. My dad and stepmom were invited to join us. That was a big deal for Marie. We watched the Packers play Detroit on her new big screen plasma TV. My father and Marie did not have a very outwardly loving relationship. They would argue. I would say to him, way to go, pick on the girl with cancer. He would say she doesn't look sick. At least they both rooted for Green Bay.

Picture this, it was on Marie's bucket list to go deer hunting with her grandpa. It was very early, before light. I went to my usual tree stand. that I went to every time I went. They sat together in Dad's deer blind for must have been three hours. They of course saw nothing. Marie still wanted to shoot the gun at a target I set up. The lid to a five-gallon bucket. Marie swung her shotgun around as she turned, and it pointed in Dad's direction. Even though there was no round in the chamber, he went totally off on her as if she were going to shoot him. This was his way of teaching her some gun safety. Marie handed me the shotgun and walked away. I chambered the round and shot a hole right through the center of the bucket lid. Dad then fired a round at the lid and put his round at the rim of the same lid, nearly missing it all together. Scratch that bucket list item.

Again, that year, we all drove through some of the most intense weather to Grandmother's (my mom) house for

Christmas. The whole family was there including my sister and her family, the ones who had the dairy farm, my brother and his family from New Orleans, and my other brother from down Madison way. Darling and I went up to Michigan to spend a couple days with her family and met back at mom's house for Christmas Eve day.

We all went to Grandpa's for fun in the snow and a big bonfire. Marie played in the snow, went snowmobiling with her cousins and tumbled down the hill on the saucer with her aunt and cousins.

The next day we had a Christmas feast at my sister's. Everything was perfect. We ate lots of food, drank lots of drinks, opened gifts and everyone got along. Marie bonded with her cousin, and they made a snowman. This was going to be Marie's last holiday with my side of the family.

Just one week before I was going to sign closing papers and commit to a thirty-year mortgage on the house in Rock Island, the job I asked for in Colorado Springs came through. Marie had been to visit me in Rock Island. I showed her around the town. So, I asked Marie if she wanted to live in Rock Island. She said it wasn't about living in Rock Island. She didn't want to die in Rock Island. I choked on that for a minute, then I asked her if she wanted to move to Colorado. She asked if she could see the world from the top of a mountain.

The decision was too easy. I was able to get released from the mortgage contract on the house in Rock Island. The house failed the Radon Gas test thanks to the home inspection required by the mortgage company. I said goodbye and God bless to my co-workers, moved out of my extended stay hotel, it was not a Comfort Inn. I packed my truck and headed to Colorado. I finally got to be with my Darling. It had been more than two years since we first talked on the phone after I came home from Iraq. We talked about meeting halfway between New Jersey and Colorado which happened to be Rock Island, Illinois. Well, I went the extra distance thanks to Marie.

Marie had to sell her house too before she could move. It just so happened that Marie's half-brother recently got married. He and his new Bride were looking for a house. They wanted one they could live in for a while and sell later.

I put a lot of money down on that house when Marie and I bought it. I paid off Marie's second mortgage that she was using to pay for living expenses and anything she wanted to buy. Like the Kirby vacuum cleaner her boyfriend talked her into. There was a huge amount of equity in the house. I told Marie to offer it to her half-brother. She did, and they decided to buy the house from Marie. Marie only needed enough money to move her few belongings to Colorado. Her $2500.00 Cancer awareness bed and mattress and her Kirby vacuum cleaner. It was a win-win situation for both kids.

Marie followed me to Colorado four months later with her new Jeep Liberty, her two dogs, and her one cat. Our new house had a view of Pike's Peak, a perfect separate living area downstairs with a separate entrance, and huge fenced-in back yard for the dogs. Marie and I would finally be together in one place. She would have less than 18 months to live.

Marie, Darling, and I all settled into our new family home. It didn't take long for the drama to start. Just like it always had with Marie. We set some rules for the dogs and where they could puke, poop, and pee. That meant barriers between upstairs and downstairs. Which meant barriers between Marie and Me. I remodeled the entire downstairs with all new paint, carpet, and flooring. The previous owners were using the downstairs as a dog kennel for breeding dogs. Imagine that. The carpet upstairs was old, but I needed to keep it in as good a shape as I could until I could afford to replace it. The dogs were puking and pooping downstairs on the new carpeting as expected, and the gate was set up to keep them there. The first contentious issue was why can't the dogs just have access to the whole house instead of being locked in the basement. First, to be honest it wasn't like you think of basements. The house was a split level two story layout. A nice freshly carpeted family room with a fireplace and plenty of windows for sunlight, a refinished bathroom, two bedrooms, a laundry room and a huge closet that could have been a bedroom.

Marie got bored with Wii Fit and started contacting various men through her "My Face Space" home shopping network. As much as I wanted to ignore the one Bucket list item, I believe it was the most important for her at the time. Marie wanted to find love and get married before, well you know, she didn't look pretty anymore.

Strange men started showing up at the door. Sometimes they would be in the house when we came home from work. That made me a little anxious. I was not very happy about the idea that Marie would want to still live the lifestyle she had become accustomed to when she had her own apartment. I still had that old shotgun. As time went on, we had more confrontations with Marie, which led to more man shopping. One thing about brain cancer, there is no filter. That caused some friction between Marie and Darling for sure. Marie was always trying to protect me from women who came into my life.

We spent more time taking care of Marie's dogs while she spent more time going out on dates. Early one morning I woke up to the dogs wining to go out. Marie was still sleeping, at least that's what I thought. So, I got up and let them out in the back yard. At four in the morning, we had two dogs sprayed directly in the face by at least one skunk. When it came to Marie's dogs, a little thing like getting sprayed by a skunk was not part of the sales pitch when I told her we had a huge backyard.

It's a good thing Marie followed in her mother's footsteps and worked as a dog groomer when she lived in Green Bay. I didn't have any tomato juice. Marie got up in a less than gracious mood. She grabbed a bucket, the bottle of Hydrogen Peroxide and the liquid hand soap. Out to the back patio we went to bathe those stinking dogs.

Another time while Marie was out, we let the dogs out in the rain. Our back yard was a mud pit when it rained because it had a pool that was crushed and collapsed into a big low spot that turned into one big mud puddle. Those dogs ran through that mud for an hour. We just hosed them off and when Marie came home, they were exhausted. We just acted like nothing happened.

Some of the men Marie was selecting were soldiers from where I worked. That was helpful since I could easily check them out. Marie also started meeting her new dates at pool halls to see how well they could accept getting beat at pool by a girl. That was the test before she would decide to invite them into our lives. A couple times she said they got very angry. Scratch them.

One night she was home early after being "stood up" by one of her online shopping dates. Lori and I decided to go with her to a bar down the street and shoot pool. We were going to try bonding with her on her turf. We walked in and the bartender told Marie to either finish her Red Bull or throw it out. The bartender was a soldier from the fort. He was about six feet five, bald headed with big ears.

Everyone in the place treated him like some kind of war hero. He told us he spent time in Iraq and his HMMWV was hit by an IED. He said his driver was killed and he was shot in the spleen causing him to have diabetes. He also claimed he turned down the Purple Heart. I knew something about driving in Iraq and IEDs so I was ok with the guy at first. Except for turning down a purple heart. Who does that? The soldier guy also said he was an officer, a Major, and everyone in the place had the same impression. He always wore his uniform pants and just his T-Shirt. We never saw any rank on his uniform.

One night a week was Karaoke. For the first song of the night, he would sing "American Soldier" which scored him even more points. We are all impressed, and Marie started dating the war hero bartender. The bar had two pool tables Marie called Bar Boxes because they were smaller than regulation tournament nine-ball pool tables.

I wanted to send him an email at work, but his name kept coming up as a Staff Sergeant. I confronted him with that information, and he told me he was undercover working as a Staff sergeant, but he was really a Major. So now he is Major Sergeant.

One story led to another, and Marie had enough of me and Lori challenging everything he said so she moved in with

Major Sergeant. Marie lived with us less than six months and she was moving in with the Major Sergeant, War hero, and bar tender/owner. Now if Darling and I want to see or spend time with Marie, we had to be cordial, with no more questions about his identity. That was not easy for Darling. She also had little to no filter when it came to protecting people she loved and cared about.

We continued to go to the bar because Marie started working there as a bartender. And yes, they got another dog, a Basset hound. This one was trained by its master to chase Marie's new cat, John Wayne. The cat walked with a limp because it had a broken hip when she found him. It stayed in the bathroom vanity while she nursed it back to health. We tried to keep up a social life with them. We went dancing downtown. We went to the VFW out of town. We invited them for the holidays, we went out to dinner, and we spent time with Marie in the bar down the street playing pool. We even went with them on a motorcycle run to deliver toys for the Toys for Tots. They were the ones smoking while they rode in the group and peeing on the side of the road when we stopped to collect all the stragglers or wait for the police escort to bring us through town.

Christmas of 2008 was the biggest Christmas we had so far. We spent a lot of money on all the kids. Among other gifts I got Marie a full day SPA treatment at Veda's which is a very exclusive place and very expensive. We thought it would be a girl's day for Marie and Darling's daughter. She decided to exchange it for the couple's massage with Major Sergeant. They also never went. Who knows where the gift card is today. Some of my in-laws came for the week after

Christmas through New Years. They all went skiing and everyone had a great time. Marie and Major Sergeant spent less than an hour at the house.

Over the course of the following summer, things were not so great for Marie. They would get into fights, and I would go haul Marie back home. She would get a phone call and move back in with him the next day. The next full moon they would get drunk and fight, and I would haul Marie back home. One time I showed up and he had a nice shiner. All 5 '2" of her slugged all six-foot six Major Sergeant right in the kisser. Each time I would tell her to take less stuff with her when she went back. I hauled her 42" plasma TV, I bought for her in Green Bay, out of his house by myself for the second time. They are not light. I wasn't going to let it go back there again. When he came and asked for it to hang in the Bar, Darling told him to go pound sand.

They blamed alcohol and they blamed his PTSD. They said they stopped drinking so much, and the calls stopped coming. We found out that Major Sergeant was being processed out of the Army as a fully disabled vet due to his injuries and his condition. Drinking a case of Red Bull and going for an EKG works wonders when you need to trigger a pacemaker, allegedly. His stories became less believable although Darling never once believed what he was saying. We spent less time with them, and they made more of an effort to stay away from us.

Marie's 29th Birthday was more involved around her mother and her friend Missy. By that next summer Missy was having a baby. Marie spent her 29th Birthday in Atlanta with Major

Sergeant. They spent most of the time with Marie's mother who really liked Major sergeant. They also spent some time with Missy and her husband, who had less than glowing opinions about Major Sergeant. Marie's grandfather (Papa) and Missy's husband were both in the military and had their doubts.

Marie and Major Sergeant stayed away from our house for the next couple months. We would have to go to the bar to visit when we wanted to see how she was doing. Marie was now a full-time bartender, for tips. We noticed she was getting yelled at for not being able to keep the bar tabs and receipts straight. Darling and I would bite our lips and just tell her we were there for her, and walk out. It was getting too difficult to watch.

Marie spent a lot of time on the road between Colorado and upstate New York dealing with Major Sergeant's divorce, his ex-wife, I think, and his two kids. They made that trip at least twice. Besides her 30th Birthday trip to Georgia and back to Colorado.

Marie was having more trouble with her headaches and became quite belligerent at times. She would scream at people and argue over anything. She smoked a lot of cigarettes, and then smoked a lot more. She was always dropping the F-Bomb. It was difficult to be around either of them.

I started working on my own house, since we didn't have Marie living downstairs. We grew a garden, and we had a sunroom built on the deck for a hot tub. We started on the inside by planning to replace all the carpeting and flooring upstairs. We set up our new log bed that my mother built in Stepdad's wood shop. We bought some new furniture, installed some vinyl flooring and started making the house our home. We played golf at the Broadmoor in a charity tournament. We did a lot of wine tasting, and we rode our motorcycle on trips to the mountains with the neighbor.

We sort of messed up Father's Day by wanting to go for a motorcycle ride with Marie and Major Sergeant before they opened the bar on that Sunday. We were supposed to wait until after they opened the bar, but it was too beautiful outside. We were up early; we went to church, and we wanted an early start up the hill from Colorado Springs to Cripple Creek. Marie wanted me to go riding with them that afternoon to a bar near Denver they were going to check out. They thought I would like to do that for Father's Day.

After not seeing them the rest of the summer we invited them to the Grand Cayman Islands for her 30th Birthday. I wanted Marie to fly with us. They were going to drive to Atlanta, drop off the dogs at her mother's, drive to Charlotte, fly to Grand Cayman, spend the week with us, fly back to Charlotte, drive to Atlanta, spend time with her mother then drive back to Colorado. Major Sergeant was not supposed to be flying with all the ear surgery he was having due to more service-related injuries. After driving back and forth across the country three or four times, that we knew of, it was not a surprise when they changed the agenda.

The two of them drove to Atlanta where they spent a few days with Marie's mother and drove back to Colorado. Had we not asked a couple weeks before the trip if they were still going with us to the Caymans, they would not have told us. They transferred the money from the plane tickets I bought them to go on a cruise in the spring with her mother. Well, they never intended to get on that plane and Marie wasn't going to make it to the cruise.

I'm not sure what happened to the money for the plane tickets. Knowing what we know now, she really did need the time to just rest and do nothing. It was also Missy's baby's first birthday that week. Marie wanted Missy to drive the 60 miles one way to her mother's lake home to visit and then drive back that night to prepare for her child's first birthday the next day. That apparently caused a rift between Marie and Sissy that Marie's mother supported. After Sissy and her husband drove from Atlanta to Green Bay for Marie's 28th Birthday. They were angry because Missy wouldn't drive the 60 miles one way to visit with Marie, the day before her sons first Birthday. All the while this drama was going on, we were in the Caymans. Swimming with the dolphins on a vacation that Marie was supposed to be with us.

August 28th, 2009. Marie was now 30 years old. She fulfilled her promise to me. Her life seemed out of control, but I think she was ready to just give up. I could see in her eyes that she was in a daze all the time, she was getting dragged around, not knowing where she was or where she was going. On the way back to Colorado Marie got a severe headache that wouldn't quit.

We all got back to Colorado from Marie's Birthday celebrations at about the same time. On September 10th,

2009, we got a phone call from the emergency room. We rushed to the hospital. It was Memorial Central where Darling worked. Marie and Major Sergeant were sitting in the waiting room amongst about 50 people with various symptoms. Most obvious were the Swine and H1N1 flu virus. Marie's face was drooping on the right side. It appeared as if she had a stroke. She would try to smile and only half her face would respond. This was clearly an indication that something serious was going on with the left side of her brain.

She got some pain meds as we sat there for what seemed like hours before we moved to another room. We sat in the inner sanctum as Marie was processed for a CT scan. They took her away for a while, so we sat some more, waiting for her to come back. Sitting and waiting was a common activity when Marie would go into the ER. Keeping her entertained and waiting for what can only be bad news is not an easy task. Marie only wanted pain medication and to be on her way. She never wanted to know, although she already knew, and had known for a long time.

When the ER doctor arrived back at our room, he didn't know who to tell or how to deliver news this bad. I walked outside the room with him and explained the situation. That I had been waiting for this to happen for about four years. I told him I knew there was a tumor, and it was going to eventually kill her. He was relieved. When I looked at the CT scan with the doctor I almost went into shock. I knew what was going to happen, but I didn't think it would be right now. I asked his opinion about how much longer, even though it was obvious.

He wanted to wait for the neurosurgeon and the MRI results the next day before making any predictions. So, Marie spent the night in the hospital until morning when she got her MRI results. I spoke with the neurologist. He looked at the MRI and said there was nothing he could do. He said it would probably be single digit weeks to a few months. I could be optimistic, but the signs seemed to indicate the former. On 9/11/09 Marie begins the most difficult journey of her life.

We talked to the nurse and got us a copy of the MRI. We talked Marie into taking some steroids to reduce her brain swelling or she was going to have a seizure and go into a coma. Over the next day they had her on steroids and a morphine drip. They rather quickly weaned her off steroids and by the following day she ripped out her IV and left the hospital. She was assigned a resident doctor as her primary care physician. He basically prescribed morphine, anti-seizure medication, and Hospice. I took the hospice information and all the forms to get Marie some financial assistance and get her officially out of the hospital.

Marie's mother arrived the next day. Marie had nine weeks and six days to live. Single Digit maximum.

Marie was still on Morphine and weaning off the steroids, but she wanted to get new glasses. It was a tradition for me to take Marie for new glasses when she needed them. She was still loopy and couldn't fill out the paper on the clipboard. She put her house address from Green Bay, Her city from Colorado and her zip code from Georgia. She handed the clipboard to Major Sergeant, and he filled it out for her. She practically stumbled into the exam room. I 'm sure she was a challenge for the eye doctor. Then she tried on every pair of glasses in the store. I don't know why we didn't just start with the most expensive pair, since that is the pair she picked out.

While Marie was preoccupied, we discussed her desire to have an advanced directive not to resuscitate if she started to go into cardiac arrest. Or if they tried to put her on life support. She already had her Last Will and Testament. I already knew what to do with her estate. I had one of those home legal software programs, so I gave it to her to do the advanced directive.

Marie's mother was in town now, staying at Major Sergeant's house. I went to work that Monday. By the time I got home that Monday afternoon, Marie called me and said she was married. They were celebrating at the bar. She asked if I could come there to join them. The selling point of the marriage was that Major Sergeant took her last name so she wouldn't have broken her promise to me. And now all her medical bills would be paid by the government under Tri-Care. Bonus, is that he would get SGLI Life insurance to pay for any additional expenses. She already had Medicare. Her bills were already paid by the government.

First her mother witnessed and signed the advanced directive. I was not at the wedding so I could not object or forever hold my peace. Then her mother witnessed and signed her new Will and Testament which gave everything to Major Sergeant Weaver, her new husband.

I called Hospice that day to make sure someone contacted Marie. I explained the situation, so Hospice was ready to support Marie. Once they found out Marie was married, they told me they were focused on her husband and not what her mother or I wanted. Major Sergeant Weaver was now the primary caregiver. I asked Hospice if they thought she was of sound mind at the time she signed, and they witnessed her directive and Will. The Hospice representative said her mother also witnessed the advanced directive and Marie looked ok to her when she signed it. Who wouldn't believe the mother?

She said Major Sergeant was very knowledgeable about the drugs and the regiment for dispensing the morphine. Two days earlier she had a CT scan that showed a banana sized tumor in her brain, she was on morphine for two days, and just the day before, she couldn't fill out a form at the eye doctor. Darling and I were not consulted or asked to attend the wedding ceremony even though I was at work only five minutes away.

All the remaining activities occurred at Major Sergeant Weaver's house and were centered around her new husband as the primary caregiver, and now, beneficiary. She wouldn't change her name, so he changed his, as a selling point for dad to accept her getting married. Once again, I was so proud. Marie insisted that she loved Major Sergeant Weaver, and she trusted him to take care of her until the end. Marie's mother embraced Marie's new husband as her one and only ever to be son-in-law. She defended him when I would go on the offensive. That only jeopardized my chances to see Marie at his house. So, I went along with the charade. Besides, this isn't about him, it is about Marie, but I am telling the story. Maybe they have a different version in their book about Marie.

On a light note. He left Marie and me home alone to dispense candy bars on Halloween that year. Marie loved Halloween. I have a wonderful record of our Halloween history from when she was as young as three until fright night on the porch in New Jersey. We gave away all the boxes of buy a candy bar for charity that Major Sergeant was supposed to sell at the Bar. Word must have gotten out because we had a line at the door.

For the next nine weeks I would work half days or sit with Marie so her husband could go to the bar and do paperwork, train his new Bartender, or take money to the bank. Marie's mother traveled back and forth from Atlanta. She would stay with Marie, so Marie's husband didn't have to care for Marie by himself. Hospice would show up and care for the distraught husband as they dropped off more morphine.

Marie deteriorated quickly. She wanted her own bed from my house that she and I bought. It was a very expensive pillow-top with cancer awareness ribbons quilted into the top. I hated to bring it there, but Marie was dying, and she wanted her bed. Her husband was very vocal about how he hated that bed because it gave him a sore back. He said he would not sleep on it. I figure he wasn't interested in sleeping with Marie any longer either. Then they brought the shower seat and then they brought the bedside toilet. Eventually they would bring the hospital bed.

Marie would constantly fight the effects of the morphine and constantly fight us for trying to help her. She loved to sit in front of the fireplace and watch movies while the dogs fought with each other or chased the cat. There was often a hot fire in the fireplace, and she was very content watching Christmas movies. She also watched all the ghost hunting shows and some explicit movies about dying. One day I suggested we get her a tree and decorate it for an early Christmas. Marie's husband went all out and bought one of those cheap little fiber optic trees at Wal-Mart. He meticulously set it in front of the fireplace. That reminded me of a Christmas a while back in Seattle.

We grew some pumpkins in our garden, so we picked out the nicest one and brought it to her for Halloween. I sat with Marie on Halloween while Major Sergeant Weaver went to the bar, to train his new bartender. He left Marie and me home alone to dispense candy. We gave away all the buy a candy bar for charity Major Sergeant was supposed to sell at the Bar. Word must have gotten out because we had a line at the door.

I handed out candy while Marie slept in front of the fire. That is about the time I asked friends and family to send some cards and letters. They were all perfect and I made sure they were set up on the bar in the dingy smoky basement where Marie would spend her last days. Marie received a single bouquet of flowers. It was from her half-brother. We received a plant from my youngest brother that we still have 15 years later. My older brother sent the most wonderful crystal candle holders that were set on the table with Marie's urn just below our picture of the Last Supper.

I asked Missy if she wanted to come and spend some time with Marie in Colorado. When I mentioned it to Marie and Marie's mother, you would think I asked Kennedy to have a beer with Castro. Marie and her mother were still upset over the Georgia trip when Missy wouldn't come to see Marie at the lake house on her 29th Birthday. I basically said hell with it and flew Missy to Colorado. Missy and the newlyweds went out on the town. Marie played pool and cut up with Missy just like old times. I believe it's what they call the last surge of life and energy before they crash. That was the last time Marie left the house until the funeral home came to get her.

Marie's mother and grandmother from Georgia came to stay with Marie. Marie's Aunt and uncle from New Hampshire came to stay. My mother came and stayed with us to see Marie one last time.

We had some early winter weather that November, but every day I would get out of work at noon and drive to that dreaded house. I would sit in that smoky basement and watch Marie struggle to light a cigarette, dribble drinks and food on herself or just lay there and sleep. Her waking hours were confusion, disoriented and she could no longer stand on her own, nor could she put a sentence together. I believe the last coherent discussion she had was an appointment she requested with Darling. Marie said she trusted Darling with me and asked her to promise to take care of me.

Marie's husband just kept giving her morphine according to his regimented schedule and dosage. Up until the last few days she fought everyone who tried to help her. She would stand up and fall. She would fall off the toilet or not even make it that far. About the only pleasure she had was when my Darling would take time to help her bathe, then wash and comb her hair. Every day her husband would tell us exactly what was going to happen next as if he were an expert. The internet has sites with information that will tell you exactly what will happen and when as a person is dying from brain cancer. He had all the websites up on Marie's computer along with her Face Book and My Space sites.

On November 18th, 2009, I was very slow about getting out of work to go see Marie. I stopped at home to change clothes. I changed my clothes and started driving over to their house. It was almost noon. The traffic was exceptionally heavy. I had to stop for every light. Every car in front of me was going below the speed limit. It was freezing, the wind was blowing, the road was icy. I pulled up in front of the house and began reading some email on my work Blackberry. Marie's aunt came out of the house and yelled for me to hurry. That moment was the first time I hurried all day. I ran into the house and downstairs where Marie's mother was standing, next to the hospice bed where Marie was lying. Marie only lasted a few days in her own bed before Hospice brought their bed in, so Marie could stay "in the basement".

I knelt next to Marie and held her hand. Her eyes were closed, and her breathing was nearly non-existent. Her mother held her other hand but was yelling for Marie's Aunt to call Major Sergeant Weaver and get him there right away. He wasn't there because he had said earlier that he was in a bad place and needed to get out of the house. I placed my open palm on Marie's forehead and held her hand as she gasped her last breath. I told her that I loved her, as tears just streamed down my face.

Suddenly Marie sat up, her eyes opened, she was staring, not at me, or her mother, but into the distance, as if she were looking at a familiar place or familiar face. I could see that she wasn't, but I told her not to be afraid. Then as if someone was holding her from behind, she slowly closed her eyes and gently laid back down. She was gone. I held her hand and kept my other hand on her forehead until her temperature began to cool. I was relieved that she wasn't there anymore.

Just then Marie's uncle said, "it might be a good idea to move to the other side of the bed for when Marie's husband arrived", so I wouldn't be in his way. She was gone and he wasn't there. I could let that whole concept go for now. I stayed until the funeral home people came and took her withered beat-up body away. I watched until the van turned the corner down the street and faded out of sight.

There is so much more to Marie's story and so much more to the ending. Marie's widowed husband, Major Sergeant Weaver, I was told Married the Bartender he was training the day Marie died, allegedly. He sold the house, he collects half of Marie's social security, he got all her disability life insurance, and whatever the Army pays in life insurance for the death of a spouse these days. Marie wanted him to keep and take care of her new Jeep and not buy another new Jeep. He bought the new Jeep almost immediately after she died. He was rear ended in it. I bet he called Frank Azar, the personal injury lawyer. I am also wondering if his new bride has a terminal illness. Or, if he will show up at my funeral now and claim he is the sole living survivor. He may not get that old shotgun, but he may get one or two of the shells.

The last time I spoke with Marie's mother she said the dogs were doing fine but costing a lot of money. I believe Marie expected some of the insurance money to go towards her critters in her First Will and Testament, that I helped her write. That Will was revoked when her mother and the hospice lady witnessed Marie's second Last Will and Testament. Just as Marie and I planned four years earlier I was able to salvage some of the money in our joint checking account. I closed the account just before we went to the funeral home.

While at the funeral home Marie's mother handed me Marie's checkbook and asked me to sign a check from our closed account to pay for the cremation and viewing from her estate. They claimed my joint account with Marie from Green Bay, that paid her mortgage, and her car insurance was considered Marie's estate.

The two of them spent some time trying to figure out what to have inscribed on their urns for Marie. For me it was a no-brainer. I have some of Marie's ashes in an urn I bought at the funeral home price, with my own money, and it has Marie's own poem inscribed on the front of it. The Urn Marie's husband picked out was discovered in a storage unit three years later. Where they bid on the contents at auction. All of Marie's stuff was in that storage unit except for a few things I still had left from our old house, which all burned in the Black Forest, Colorado forest fire. The purchaser of the contents was nice enough to contact the mortuary. They were able to find me, not Major Sergeant, and not her mother. All I got was Marie's ashes in the urn he bought on the internet to save money, so I sent the urn to Missy.

Understanding

Longer roads have been taken with shorter breaths. Weary minds wander when rendered souls begin to rest. Mistakes are made when thoughts enter our imaginative minds. Loneliness is captured by our hearts and not so hard to find. Pondering over the purpose of our painful existence, words linger in the air, with knowledge at a distance. I cannot comprehend the penalty or demand for purity and love that which none understand. Searching for a world of honor, dignity, and respect, we experience nothing but hate heartache and neglect. Knowing nothing at all is everything to me. For he who knows everything has nothing left to see. I leave you here with one final thought: Those who never suffered, never really fought.

Lindsy "Marie" Weaver

www.ingramcontent.com/pod-product-compliance
Lightning Source LLC
Chambersburg PA
CBHW051538120626
46551CB00013B/1269